Software Engineering Institute
Carnegie Mellon

Ultra-Large-Scale Systems

The Software Challenge of the Future

June 2006

Pittsburgh, PA 15213-3890

This report was prepared for the

SEI Administrative Agent
ESC/XPK
5 Eglin Street
Hanscom AFB, MA 01731-2100

This work is sponsored by the U. S. Army. The Software Engineering Institute is a federally funded research and development center sponsored by the U. S. Department of Defense.

For information about purchasing paper copies of SEI reports, please visit the publications portion of our Web site:
http://www. sei.cmu.edu/publications/pubweb. html

Table of Contents

Table of Contents

List of Tables

Acknowledgments

The principal team of authors who wrote this report consists of Peter Feiler, John Goodenough, Rick Linger, Tom Longstaff, Rick Kazman, Mark Klein, Linda Northrop, and Kurt Wallnau from the Carnegie Mellon® Software Engineering Institute (SEI), along with Richard P. Gabriel, Sun Microsystems, Inc.; Douglas Schmidt, Vanderbilt University; and Kevin Sullivan, University of Virginia.

The team thanks the many individuals who contributed directly to its work.

The Ultra-Large-Scale (ULS) Systems Study Team consisted of Gregory Abowd, Georgia Institute of Technology; Carliss Baldwin, Harvard Business School; Robert Balzer, Teknowledge Corporation; Gregor Kiczales, University of British Columbia; John Lehoczky, Carnegie Mellon University; Ali Mili, New Jersey Institute of Technology; Peter Neumann, SRI International; Mark Pleszkoch, SEI; Mary Shaw, Carnegie Mellon University; Daniel Siewiorek, Carnegie Mellon University; and Jack Whalen, Palo Alto Research Center (PARC). All of these individuals made substantive contributions to the foundational ideas that the author team developed in this report.

Invited speakers at an early meeting were Assistant Secretary of the Army Claude Bolton (on video), Office of the Assistant Secretary of the U. S. Army (Acquisition, Logistics, & Technology) (ASA ALT); Peter Freeman, National Science Foundation; David Emery, DSI; and Bruce Krogh, Carnegie Mellon University. They provided valuable inspiration to the study principals.

This report was reviewed in draft form by individuals chosen for their diverse perspectives and technical expertise. The purpose of this independent review was to elicit candid and critical comments that would help make the published report as technically sound as possible. The author team is grateful to those who carefully and thoughtfully reviewed its interim drafts: John Bay, Air Force Research Lab; Brian Barry, Bederra Corporation; Barry Boehm, University of Southern California; Larry Druffel, South Carolina Research Authority (SCRA); Peter Freeman, National Science Foundation; Ron Goldman, Sun Microsystems Laboratories; Watts S. Humphrey, SEI; Bruce Krogh, Carnegie Mellon University; Jim Linnehan, ASA ALT; Martin Rinard, Massachusetts Institute of Technology; Dennis Smith, SEI; and Guy Steele, Sun Microsystems, Inc.

Although these reviewers provided many constructive comments and suggestions, they were not asked to endorse the final conclusions or recommendations presented in this report, nor did they see the final draft of the report before its release. Responsibility for the final content of this report rests entirely with the author team.

The author team is also grateful for support provided by SEI staff: David Carney, Suzanne Couturiaux, Pamela Curtis, David Gregg, Laura Huber, Bob Krut, Melissa Neely, Ray Obenza, Daniel Pipitone, Bill Pollak, Hal Stevens, Pennie Walters, Sharon West, Barbara White, David White, David Zubrow, and the SEI Information Technology staff.

Executive Summary

The U. S. Department of Defense (DoD) has a goal of information dominance—to achieve and exploit superior collection, fusion, analysis, and use of information to meet mission objectives. This goal depends on increasingly complex systems characterized by thousands of ***platforms,***[1] sensors, decision nodes, weapons, and warfighters connected through heterogeneous wired and wireless networks. These systems will push far beyond the size of today's systems and ***systems of systems*** by every measure: number of lines of code; number of people employing the system for different purposes; amount of data stored, accessed, manipulated, and refined; number of connections and interdependencies among software components; and number of hardware elements. They will be ***ultra-large-scale (ULS) systems***.

The sheer scale of ULS systems will change everything. ULS systems will necessarily be decentralized in a variety of ways, developed and used by a wide variety of stakeholders with conflicting needs, evolving continuously, and constructed from heterogeneous parts. People will not just be users of a ULS system; they will be elements of the system. Software and hardware failures will be the norm rather than the exception. The acquisition of a ULS system will be simultaneous with its operation and will require new methods for control. These characteristics are beginning to emerge in today's DoD systems of systems; in ULS systems they will dominate. Consequently, ULS systems will place unprecedented demands on software acquisition, production, deployment, management, documentation, usage, and evolution practices.

Fundamental gaps in our current understanding of software and software development at the scale of ULS systems present profound impediments to the technically and economically effective achievement of the DoD goal of deterrence and dominance based on information superiority. These gaps are strategic, not tactical. They are unlikely to be addressed adequately by incremental research within established categories. Rather, we require a broad new conception of both the nature of such systems and new ideas for how to develop them. We will need to look at them differently, not just as systems or systems of systems, but as ***socio-technical ecosystems.*** We will face fundamental challenges in the design and evolution, orchestration and control, and monitoring and assessment of ULS systems. These challenges require *breakthrough* research.

1 ***Bold-italic*** formatting of a word or phrase indicates that its definition appears in the Glossary.

We propose a ULS systems research agenda for an interdisciplinary portfolio of research in at least the following areas:

- **Human Interaction:** involves anthropologists, sociologists, and social scientists conducting detailed socio-technical analyses of user interactions in the field, with the goal of understanding how to construct and evolve such socio-technical systems effectively.
- **Computational Emergence:** explores the use of methods and tools based on economics and ***game theory*** (e.g., ***mechanism design***) to ensure globally optimal ULS system behavior and explores ***metaheuristics*** and ***digital evolution*** to augment the cognitive limits of human designers.
- **Design:** broadens the traditional technology-centric definition of design to include people and organizations; social, cognitive, and economic considerations; and design structures such as ***design rules*** and government policies.
- **Computational Engineering:** focuses on evolving the expressiveness of representations to accommodate the semantic diversity of many languages and focuses on providing automated support for computing the evolving behavior of components and their compositions.
- **Adaptive System Infrastructure:** investigates integrated development environments and runtime platforms that will support the decentralized nature of ULS systems as well as technologies, methods, and theories that will enable ULS systems to be developed in their deployment environments.
- **Adaptable and Predictable System Quality:** focuses on how to maintain quality in a ULS system in the face of continuous change, ongoing failures, and attacks and focuses on how to identify, predict, and control new indicators of ***system health*** (akin to the U. S. gross domestic product) that are needed because of the scale of ULS systems.
- **Policy, Acquisition, and Management:** focuses on transforming acquisition policies and processes to accommodate the rapid and continuous evolution of ULS systems by treating suppliers and supply chains as intrinsic and essential components of a ULS system.

The proposed research does not supplant current, important software research but rather significantly expands its horizons. Moreover, because we are focused on systems of the future, we have purposely avoided couching our descriptions in terms of today's technology. The envisioned outcome of the proposed research is a spectrum of technologies and methods for developing these systems of the future, with national-security, economic, and societal benefits that extend far beyond ULS systems themselves.

Though our research agenda does not prescribe a single, definitive roadmap, we offer three structures that suggest ways to cluster and prioritize groups of research areas mapping the research areas and topics to (1) specific DoD missions and required capabilities, (2) DoD research funding types required to support them, and (3) estimates of the relative starting points of the research. These structures can then be used to define one or more roadmaps that could lead to one or more ULS systems research programs or projects.

As a first step, we recommend the funding and establishment of a ULS System Research Startup Initiative, which over the course of the next two years would, among other things,

- work with others to conduct new basic research in key areas;
- foster the growth of a community of informed stakeholders and researchers; and
- formulate and issue an initial Broad Agency Announcement (BAA) to attract researchers with proven expertise in the diverse set of disciplines (e.g., software engineering, economics, human factors, cognitive psychology, sociology, systems engineering, and business policy) that are collectively required to meet the challenge of ULS systems.

The United States needs a program that will fund the software research required to sustain ongoing transformations in national defense and achieve the DoD goal of information dominance. The key challenge is the decision to move forward. The ULS System Research Agenda presented in this report provides the starting point for the path ahead.

Part I

1 Introduction

1.1 Genesis of the ULS Systems Research Study

The office of the Assistant Secretary of the U. S. Army (Acquisition, Logistics, & Technology) (ASA ALT) funded the Software Engineering Institute (SEI) to lead a 12-month investigation of ultra-large-scale (ULS) systems software. ASA ALT posed this question to the SEI: "Given the issues with today's software engineering, how can we build the systems of the future that are likely to have billions of lines of code?"

The intended outcome of the study was a proposed research agenda for ULS systems; a proposal for a program that would fund, coordinate, and conduct needed research; and the creation of a collaborative research network that would work toward solving the ULS system problem for the U. S. Department of Defense (DoD).

Although a billion lines of code was the initial challenge, increased code size brings with it increased scale in many other dimensions, posing challenges that strain current software foundations. To understand the challenges and the research needed to meet them, the study brought together software experts and experts from outside the software engineering field from a variety of institutions and organizations. This multi-disciplinary team sought solutions both within and beyond traditional software and systems engineering disciplines. This report describes and justifies the ULS system research agenda that resulted from the year-long study.

To appreciate the need for the study and the value of its output, it is important to first understand current DoD objectives and to analyze the fundamental shortfalls in today's software concepts, tools, and methods for reaching those objectives.

1 Introduction

1.2 The DoD's Goal of Information Dominance

The DoD has a goal of information dominance—to achieve and exploit superior collection, fusion, analysis, and use of information to meet mission objectives. As articulated in the recent *Quadrennial Defense Review Report,*[2] achievement of this goal depends on increasingly complex systems characterized by thousands of ***platforms***, sensors, decision nodes, weapons, and warfighters connected through heterogeneous wired and wireless networks. These systems will be ULS systems. The Global Information Grid (GIG), the Army Future Combat Systems (FCS), and FORCEnet are examples of emerging DoD ***systems of systems*** intended to organize and coordinate this large human, application, and technology space to

- provide DoD planners with the right information at the right place and the right time across a range of support systems and battlefield systems;
- optimally and adaptively manage information resources to provide usable target-quality information to warfighters engaged in tactical operations; and
- conduct effective information operations even in the face of attack, while also denying information critical to adversaries.

This technology base must be capable of orchestrating the human, computing, and communications environment to aggregate, filter, and prioritize the delivery of this information to work effectively in the context of transient and enduring resource constraints and failures. An essential property of information dominance is continuous adaptation. Adaptation is needed to compensate for changes in the mission requirements (such as rerouting strike packages to engage time-critical targets and modifying target/weapon pairings to avoid fratricide) and operating environments (such as dynamic network topologies, publish/subscribe membership changes, and intermittent connectivity).

1.3 The Missing Key to Information Dominance

Although systems comprise far more than software, it is software that fundamentally makes possible the achievement of the DoD goal of information dominance and the envisioned improvement in human and organizational performance. At the same time, though, software also presents the greatest impediment to DoD goals.

We have seen transformations in all facets of society that have been catalyzed by advances in software technology. The revolution in business practices effected by Google, for example, is directly traceable to advances in software technology—specifically, new algorithms that enable a scalable architecture for information searches.

2 *Quadrennial Defense Review Report,* February 2006, http://www.defenselink.mil/qdr/report/Report20060203.pdf

Yet, from the perspective of the underlying science and engineering knowledge base, software is the least well understood and the most problematic element of large-scale systems. *Software* and software project failures are among the dominant causes of *system* cost and schedule overruns; of failures of *systems* to satisfy the requirements of those who procure and use them; and, increasingly, of costly and dangerous *system* failures. Despite the careful application of modern software engineering techniques, software failure is far more prevalent than hardware failure as a cause of major system outages. While some problems are caused by poor practice, the root cause of most system problems is our inadequate software knowledge base.

1.4 The Engineering Perspective on Software Development

The problems presented by software have long been recognized. By the late 1960s, it was clear that the software problem was real, significant, and growing rapidly. The NATO Conference held in 1968 was a watershed event.[3] At that conference, the community agreed to characterize software development as an *engineering* problem and to establish as a goal that the computer science research and development community solve the major open problems by working to establish a new theoretical and practical discipline of *software engineering*.

In the nearly 40 years since 1968, tremendous progress has been made in the field of software engineering. The net effect has made it possible to construct increasingly complex systems. At the same time, as our software engineering capabilities have grown, so have our aspirations, and our aspirations continue to largely exceed our capabilities. That is, with respect to current large software-intensive systems, our aspiration to establish software development as an engineering discipline is, *to a significant extent,* still an aspiration. As we struggle to develop today's systems, we simultaneously aspire to develop the far more ambitious systems that we envision for the future.

The President's Information Technology Advisory Committee (PITAC) clearly stated that our current software science and technology base is inadequate to meet current and future needs;[4] blue-ribbon panels have identified major problems in software development as challenge problems in computer science; and reports such as that by the Standish Group[5] document an unimpressive record in large software projects in the private sector—even in the relatively well-understood domain of business applications. In the Standish Group's most recent report, only 34% of all projects were deemed to be successful.

3 Naur, P. & Randell, B. (eds.). *Software Engineering: Report of a Conference Sponsored by the NATO Science Committee*, Garmisch, Germany, 7-11 Oct. 1968, Brussels, Scientific Affairs Division, NATO (1969).

4 The President's Information Technology Advisory Committee. *Information Technology: Investing in Our Future*, final report. February 1999.

5 Standish Group. *The Chaos Report*, 2003.

1 Introduction

Although this success rate was considered a significant improvement from the 1994 rate of 16%, it is still far from adequate. The record of large government-sponsored projects is similarly lamentable; many multi-billion-dollar failures have been documented in the open literature.[6]

Today, as the evidence clearly shows, in software we continue to accept failure rates, quality problems, and costs that would be unacceptable in any other field of engineering. The software needed to achieve the DoD's goal of information dominance will be orders of magnitude more complex than that for even the most demanding of our currently existing systems. Our current practices are already extraordinarily costly and problematic; they simply will not scale to the size and levels of complexity of the ULS systems that the DoD needs in the future.

The problem that the DoD now faces is clear. *Fundamental gaps in our understanding of software and software development at the scale of ULS systems present profound impediments to the technically and economically effective achievement of the DoD goal of deterrence and dominance based on information superiority.*

1.5 The Need for a New Perspective

ULS systems will place unprecedented demands on software acquisition, production, deployment, management, documentation, usage, and evolution practices. The inability of current practices to meet these demands calls for *breakthrough* research in concepts, methods, and tools.

This report presents a new perspective on problem formulations and an initial research agenda that we believe has the potential to lead to the required breakthroughs. What this report avoids is any suggestion that adequate solutions will be found solely by a straightforward extrapolation from today's technology, including high-visibility concepts such as ***service-oriented architectures*** and model-based development. The depth of the gaps in current knowledge demands not just the incremental extension of existing work but also *innovation*, ranging from new conceptual models of the problem space to revolutionary solution approaches.

There is, without question, a critical need for a significant increase in software engineering research; but this alone will be inadequate. We need to shift our perspective and how we characterize the problems that we face. We need new ideas on how to address these problems. In many cases, such new perspectives and solution approaches will be inspired by work emerging at the intersection of traditional software engineering and other disciplines, such

6 See, for example Neumann, P. G. *Computer-Related Risks.* New York: ACM Press and Reading, MA: Addison-Wesley, 1995; Defense Science Board. *Report of the Defense Science Board Task Force on Information Warfare Defense (IW-D).* Washington, DC: Office of the Under Secretary of Defense for Acquisition and Technology, November 21, 1996; and http://www.csl.sri.com/users/neumann/illustrative.html#7.

as ***microeconomics***, biology, city planning, and anthropology—fields concerned with people as well as with coherence in the context of scale and complexity.

1.6 From Engineering to Complex Systems

Alan Kay[7] famously said that the right perspective is worth 80 IQ points.[8] For 40 years, we have embraced the traditional engineering perspective. The basic premise underlying the research agenda presented in this document is that beyond certain complexity thresholds, a traditional centralized engineering perspective is no longer adequate nor can it be the primary means by which ultra-complex systems are made real. Electrical and water systems are engineered, but cities are not—although their forms are regulated by both natural and imposed constraints. Firms are engineered, but the overall structure of the economy is not—although it is regulated. ***Ecosystems*** exhibit high degrees of complexity and organization, but not through engineering. The protocols on which the Internet is based were engineered, but the Web as a whole was not engineered—although its form is constrained by both natural and artificial regulations. In this report, we take the position that the advances needed for ULS systems require a change in perspective, from the satisfaction of requirements through traditional, rational, top-down engineering to their satisfaction by the regulation of complex, ***decentralized systems.***

1.6.1 From Buildings to Cities

One way to understand the difference in scale between traditional and ULS systems is to think about buildings, infrastructure systems, and cities. Designing and building most of today's large systems can be compared to designing and constructing a single, large building or a single infrastructure system (such as for power or water distribution). In contrast, ULS systems will operate at levels of complexity more similar to cities. At first it might seem that designing and building a city is simply a matter of designing and building a large number of buildings. However, cities are not conceived or built by individual organizations, but rather by the actions of many individuals acting locally over time. The form of a city is not defined in advance by specifying requirements; rather, a city emerges and changes over time through the loosely coordinated and regulated actions of many individuals. The factors that enable cities to be successful, then, include both extensive infrastructures not present in individual buildings as well as mechanisms that regulate local actions to maintain coherence without central control. These mechanisms include government organizations and policies, city planning, streets and transportation systems, communication and emergency services, and distribution of food and consumer goods, to name a few. Moreover, it is not feasible to design and build a city in one attempt. People, companies, communities, and organizations decide to build parts of cities for their own purposes. Cities grow and thrive

7 Alan Kay is, among other things, the winner of the Turing Award, the highest scientific award in the field of computer science.

8 "Predicting The Future," reproduced from *Stanford Engineering,* Volume 1, Number 1, Autumn 1989, pp. 1-6.

based on cultural and economic necessities, and, although some aspects of a city are designed and constructed in a local context, most elements that make up the essence of a city arise from more global policies and mechanisms, such as zoning laws, building codes, and economic incentives designed to encourage certain sorts of growth and construction.

Closer examination of the two design and construction problems—buildings versus cities—reveals that, although it is necessary, skill in designing and constructing buildings does not help much in designing and constructing a city. To point out just one of the major differences: every day in every city, construction is going on, repairs are taking place, modifications are being made, and yet the cities continue to function. Like cities, ULS systems will not simply be bigger systems: they will be interdependent webs of software-intensive systems, people, policies, cultures, and economics.

1.6.2 From Systems to Ecosystems

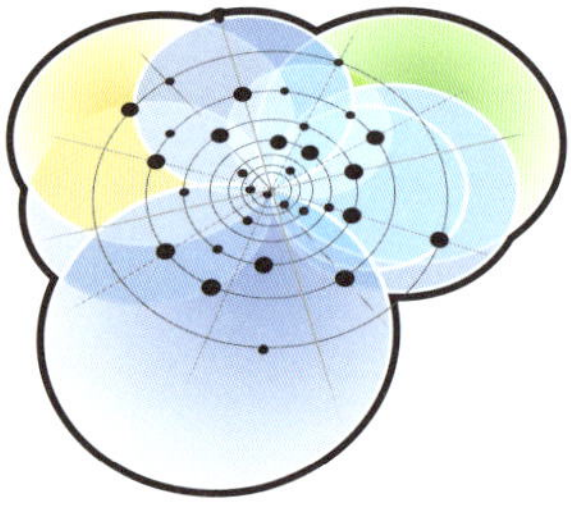

Another way to understand the needed shift in perspective is in terms of the concept of ecosystems—and of what we call ***socio-technical ecosystems*** in particular. Like a biological ecosystem, a ULS system comprises a dynamic community of interdependent and competing organisms (in this case, people, computing devices, and organizations) in a complex and changing environment. The concept of an ecosystem connotes complexity, decentralized control, hard-to-predict effects of certain kinds of disruptions, difficulty of monitoring and assessment, and the risks in ***monocultures***, as well as competition with niches, robustness, survivability, adaptability, stability, and health.

In a ULS system, there will be competition for resources, such as bandwidth, storage capacity, sensors, and weapons. The system will enforce rules intended to encourage effective use of these resources to achieve mission objectives. There may be variations in service depending on how different commanders, planners, and automated subsystems attempt to apply the available resources to missions with different levels of importance and urgency. With appropriate incentives and rules enforced by the system, these resources will be optimized so that they are appropriately available. In addition, there may be an overall measure of the ***quality of service*** being provided to different parts of the system or for different purposes (e.g., quality-of-service requirements will change for some parts of the system during a mission). This measure can be used to determine if the incentives are working as intended. As system behavior changes in response to the incentives, the incentives may also need to be changed to ensure that key mission goals are accomplished.

We traditionally view system development and acquisition as a technology-centric, rational, largely top-down, centrally controlled process of implementation and deployment. By contrast, a defining element of ULS systems is that they will include people, organizations, and technologies *at all levels*, from those responsible for overall policy implemented within the system to those producing the system to those actually using it. There will be organizations and participants responsible for setting acquisition, production, and operational *policies* governing the overall system, and there will be organizations, technologies, and people responsible for *producing* ULS systems. For example, the DoD, Congress, and the Office of the Secretary of Defense (OSD), in their roles as policy makers, will play essential roles in an overall system. Contractors and warfighters will participate at another level of system organization. There are rich kinds of interdependencies among players, systems, and activities across all of these levels.

The concept of an ecosystem is not novel. Nor is the analogy perfect. For example, unlike biological ecosystems, whose dynamics involve nutrient and energy flows, ULS ecosystem dynamics involve exchanges of economic, security, and other forms of value. Yet even with its imperfections, the analogy helps illuminate the nature of the problem facing the ULS system developer: an inadequate understanding of how to create and maintain systems that have characteristics similar to those found in ecosystems. The challenge facing the ULS systems research community is to help fill these major gaps in knowledge.

1.6.3 Beyond the Internet

The Web foreshadows the characteristics of ULS systems. Its scale is much larger than that of any of today's systems of systems. Its development, oversight, and operational control are decentralized. Its stakeholders have diverse, conflicting, complex, and changing requirements. The services it provides undergo continuous evolution. The actions of the people making use of the Web influence what services are provided, and the services provided influence the actions of people. It has been designed to avoid the worst problems deriving from the heterogeneity of its elements and to be insensitive to connection failures.

But the Web was not designed with the DoD's needs in mind. Security was not given much attention in its original design, and its use for purposes for which it was not initially intended, such as e-commerce, has revealed exploitable vulnerabilities. The elements of the Web are loosely interconnected in the sense that the failure of most elements does not have a significant effect on many users. The bandwidth available to the Web is much greater than what is likely to be available for the DoD's ULS systems. And although the Web is an important element of people's work lives, it is not as critical as a ULS DoD system would be.

1 Introduction

The existence of the Web suggests what ULS systems might be like, but despite the Web's success and ubiquity, ULS systems for DoD purposes are likely to push the boundaries of what we have learned (and are learning) from the existence of the Web.

1.7 The Results of This Study

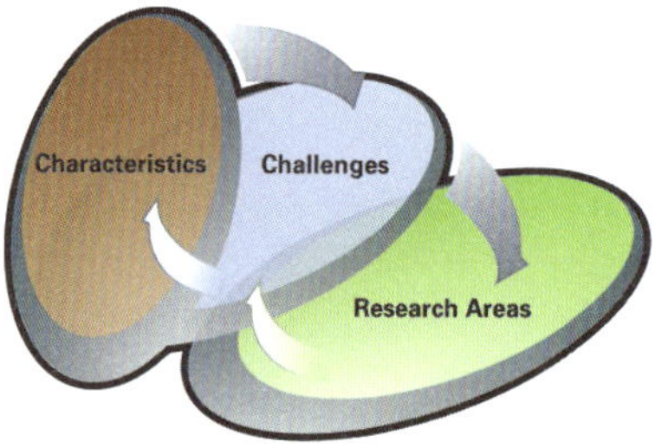

ULS System Research Agenda

The DoD's goal of information dominance, the software that will be required to achieve that goal, and the concomitant need for a new perspective in software development are all fundamental to the research agenda that resulted from our study. Our agenda is meant to catalyze a funded ULS system research program and inspire researchers from a diverse set of disciplines to address ULS system software challenges. We expect researchers to be motivated to investigate the identified topics and to propose other research in those areas. Prosecuting a research agenda of this magnitude is like planting many seeds. Some will bear fruit; others will be weeded out and perhaps substituted with heartier types. Similarly, over time we see this research agenda changing to match breakthroughs and results. We also recognize a complementary need to establish a transition component of the research program that will ensure that successful results get packaged and transitioned to the DoD as quickly as possible. The rest of this report is divided into two parts as follows:

Part I describes and justifies our ULS system research agenda.

Section 2: Characteristics of ULS Systems examines the consequences of scale implied by ULS systems. It characterizes ULS systems as complex systems that are significantly beyond the reach of the traditional engineering paradigm of software development and provides the basis for understanding the technical challenges that are inherent in these systems.

Section 3: Challenges in ULS Systems describes and analyzes the major challenges posed by ULS systems.

Section 4: Overview of Research Areas presents seven major research areas and underlying topics that hold promise for addressing ULS system challenges, thereby filling the most important gaps in software knowledge and capability at the scale needed for ULS systems.

Section 5: Summary and Recommendations shows how the proposed research topics are related to needed DoD capabilities and outlines a path forward for a substantive, long-term, funded ULS System Research Program.

Part II provides more detailed information for technically oriented readers.

Section 6: Detailed Description of Research Areas presents each research area and research topic in detail.

We also provide a **Glossary** at the end of the report. Words and phrases that are defined in the Glossary are formatted in ***bold-italic*** typeface when they appear within the text.

2
Characteristics of ULS Systems

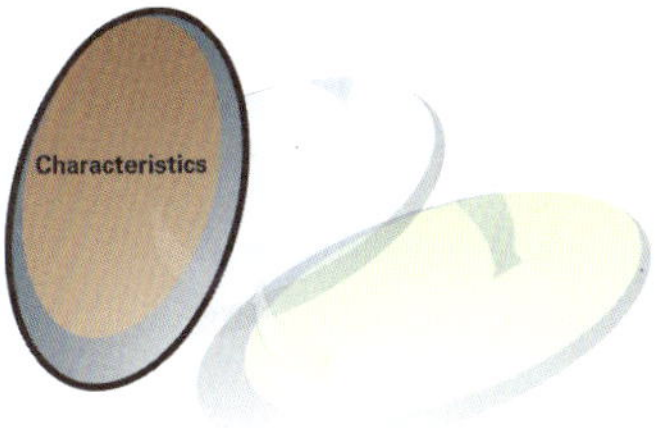

There are characteristics of ULS systems that will arise because of their scale. These characteristics undermine current, widely used, software engineering approaches and provide the basis for the technical challenges associated with ULS systems.

The primary characteristic of ULS systems is ultra-large size on any imaginable dimension—number of lines of code; number of people employing the system for different purposes; amount of data stored, accessed, manipulated, and refined; number of connections and interdependencies among software components; number of hardware elements; etc. But to understand the nature of ULS systems, we must go beyond just the concept of size; we must understand the effects of scale and the demands that ULS systems are likely to place on technologies and processes. Issues that are not significant at smaller scales become significant at ultra-large scales. The problems introduced by scale require new solution approaches and new concepts of system design, development, operation, and evolution. In short, *scale changes everything*.

ULS systems will have some characteristics in common with today's systems of systems (SoSs). Mark Maier[9] has developed a list of characteristics that distinguish large monolithic systems from systems of systems:

- **operational independence of the elements:** Component systems are independently useful.
- **managerial independence of the elements:** Component systems are acquired and operated independently; they maintain their existence independent of the SoS.
- **evolutionary development:** The SoS is not created fully formed but comes into existence gradually.

9 Maier, Mark W. *Architecting Principles for Systems-of-Systems.* http://www.infoed.com/Open/PAPERS/systems.htm, 1996.

2 Characteristics of ULS Systems

- **emergent behavior:** Behaviors of the SoS are not localized to any component system. The principal purposes of the SoS are fulfilled by these behaviors.
- **geographic distribution:** Components are so geographically distributed that their interactions are limited primarily to information exchange rather than exchanges of mass or energy.

Maier goes on to define different classes of systems of systems based on the amount of management control that is possible. The class he calls "virtual" systems of systems is closest to ULS systems:

> *Virtual systems lack a central management authority. Indeed, they lack a centrally agreed upon purpose for the system-of-systems. Large scale behavior emerges, and may be desirable, but the supersystem must rely upon relatively invisible mechanisms to maintain it.*

Maier then cites the Web and national economies as examples of virtual SoSs.

Maier's definitions are useful for classifying systems but are not so useful for understanding the underlying technical problems of ULS systems. The characteristics of ULS systems that will arise because of their scale are much more revealing. These characteristics are as follows:

- **decentralization:** The scale of ULS systems means that they will necessarily be decentralized in a variety of ways—decentralized data, development, evolution, and operational control.
- **inherently conflicting, unknowable, and diverse requirements:** ULS systems will be developed and used by a wide variety of stakeholders with unavoidably different, conflicting, complex, and changing needs.
- **continuous evolution and deployment:** There will be an increasing need to integrate new capabilities into a ULS system while it is operating. New and different capabilities will be deployed, and unused capabilities will be dropped; the system will be evolving not in phases, but continuously.
- **heterogeneous, inconsistent, and changing elements:** A ULS system will not be constructed from uniform parts: there will be some misfits, especially as the system is extended and repaired.

- **erosion of the people/system boundary:** People will not just be users of a ULS system; they will be elements of the system, affecting its overall emergent behavior.
- **normal failures:** Software and hardware failures will be the norm rather than the exception.
- **new paradigms for acquisition and policy:** The acquisition of a ULS system will be simultaneous with the operation of the system and require new methods for control.

Although these characteristics are not all independent and are already evident in some of today's largest systems, each implies a change in the fundamental assumptions that underlie today's software engineering approaches. Each contributes to the complexity of bringing ULS systems into existence, validating their behavior, and evolving their capabilities. Each derives from the consequences of scale changing everything. In the remainder of this section, we discuss each characteristic and the assumptions that the characteristic undermines. Understanding how these assumptions are undermined helps in understanding why ULS systems present new challenges and underscores the need for new research.

2.1 Decentralized Control

The scale of ULS systems will allow only limited possibilities for centralized or hierarchical control of data, development, evolution, and operation. Even the limited amount of hierarchical control that is possible today for very large systems will be challenged at the scale of ULS systems and likely require different control models.

One of today's assumptions undermined by this characteristic is the following:

All conflicts must be resolved and must be resolved uniformly. Today's systems are predicated on the idea that conflicts must be addressed and resolved. We assume that there is a conflict-resolution process and an organization that makes decisions to be followed by other elements of the system. The scale of ULS systems will make it impossible to resolve all conflicts and to resolve conflicts centrally. In an ecosystem, there is no central authority for resolving conflicts; other mechanisms serve this purpose. An ecosystem characterization of ULS systems suggests that mechanisms will be in place to resolve conflicts locally among those who have an immediate interest in the issue. Moreover, if the same conflict arises elsewhere in the system, it might be resolved differently. Today's designers of large systems generally do not consider the idea that they should tolerate conflicts or resolve the same conflict differently at different times and places. They also do not typically include procedures for determining which conflicts are of greatest importance to global ***system viability***; we have little understanding of what organizational processes work best for this purpose.

2 Characteristics of ULS Systems

2.2 Inherently Conflicting, Unknowable, and Diverse Requirements

The scale and complexity of problems to be solved by ULS systems mean that, in many cases, the requirements to be satisfied by the systems will not be adequately known until the systems are in use. Even then, as the system is put into operation, perceptions of the problem it is solving will change. Each attempt at a solution will give a deeper understanding of what the problem really is, leading to yet another attempt at a solution. Some problems addressed by ULS systems are likely to be so complex that there can be no fully satisfactory solution; requirements will never really converge.

ULS systems, by their very size and nature, will be able to serve a wide spectrum of purposes. The more a ULS system does, the more diversity and conflict it is likely to engender. Moreover, integrating solutions across this spectrum will likely require knowledge from several domains, and making use of relevant cross-domain knowledge is difficult today.

Among today's assumptions undermined by this characteristic are the following:

- **Requirements can be known in advance and change slowly as experience with a system grows.** We know that requirements for systems today are never *completely* understood in advance of building and using a system. Even so, most systems today are developed on the assumption that key requirements are sufficiently well understood that if a system is built to meet these requirements, it will be useful. But ULS systems are likely to encounter so-called ***wicked problems***[10] in which requirements are neither knowable in advance (because there is no agreement about what the problem is) nor stable (because each solution changes the problem, and no solution is considered to have "solved" the problem[11]). In ULS systems, even more so than today, system development, operation, and usage will have to be based on a premise of continual change and (re)negotiation of user needs.
- **Tradeoff decisions will be stable.** Because of the large number of ULS system users, each having different goals, different tradeoffs in system behavior may be appropriate for different groups of users, and even these tradeoffs will change over time. For example, one group may place a high value on fast response to certain types of queries, at a cost of having an increased error rate; another group may value accuracy more than responsiveness. It must be possible to configure the system as it appears to specific groups of users so that both requirements can be met simultaneously. Although we sometimes give attention to the idea that certain tradeoff decisions will have to be revised over the life of the system, we

10 Rittel, H. & Webber, M. "Dilemmas in a General Theory of Planning," pp 155-169, *Policy Sciences*, Vol. 4, Elsevier Scientific Publishing Company, Inc., Amsterdam, 1973; also http://en.wikipedia.org/wiki/Wicked_problems

11 "Wicked problems have incomplete, contradictory, and changing requirements; and solutions to them are often difficult to recognize as such because of complex interdependencies." http://en.wikipedia.org/wiki/Wicked_problems

do not generally build systems today with the idea that the system can be readily reconfigured to support different tradeoffs for different users.

2.3 Continuous Evolution and Deployment

Another consequence of size is that ULS systems will be in service for a long time. Their size will make it impractical to replace or retire them. Instead, like very large systems today, they will continuously evolve to meet new and modified requirements and to incorporate new technologies. But we envision a different type of evolution than is typical of today's very large systems. By *evolution*, we mean change that is guided and constrained by rules and policies that allow local needs to be satisfied in local ways without destroying the integrity and value of the overall system. The evolution of a ULS system will be supported by different subgroups of stakeholders, each subgroup seeking to achieve a solution that fits its own needs, but under the guidance of general economic, technical, and political rules that limit the impact (both positive and negative) of any given change.

One of today's assumptions undermined by this characteristic is the following:

System improvements are introduced at discrete intervals (build-use-build). As with cities, ULS systems must continue to function despite ongoing, simultaneous construction, repairs, improvements, and demolitions. For cities, we have considerable experience in determining how to make improvements without catastrophically interfering with the needs of the inhabitants. For most systems today, we do not typically allow different subgroups to make changes simultaneously. In ULS systems, however, the introduction of ***concurrent*** changes will generally be necessary because waiting to sequence all changes will unacceptably delay the introduction of needed capabilities and problem fixes. A key issue will be to know which changes can be made concurrently and which must be coordinated.

2 Characteristics of ULS Systems

2.4 Heterogeneous, Inconsistent, and Changing Elements

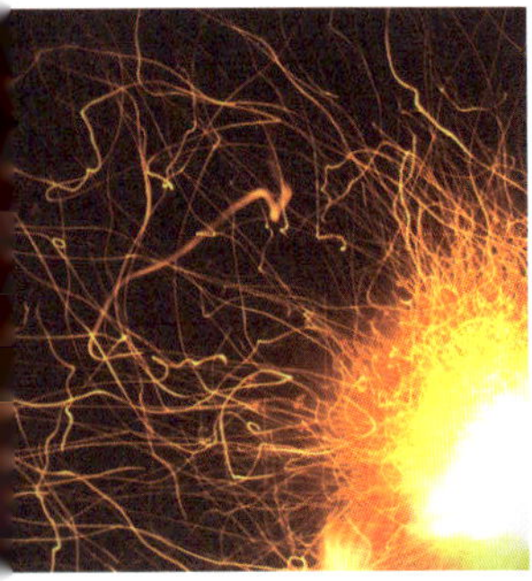

The size of a ULS system also means that its elements (i.e., its hardware, its software, its procedures and rules, its people, etc.) will be heterogeneous, inconsistent, and changing.

Heterogeneous: Software elements will be heterogeneous in part because they will come from a variety of sources. Parts of the system will be written in different languages, tuned for different hardware/software platforms, and designed according to different philosophies and methodologies. Many software elements will originate in legacy systems, written long before the first ULS system comes into existence. Some will be dynamically supplied and assimilated. Many will be services that will be provided over the Internet. A key aspect of ULS system design, construction, and evolution will entail integrating and compensating for such heterogeneous elements and engineering perspectives.

Heterogeneity can also be a benefit. In heterogeneous systems, not all elements are equally vulnerable to failures or attacks.

Inconsistent: With software originating in different places and being created and modified by dispersed teams with different schedules, processes, goals, and stakeholders, a ULS system will necessarily be composed of different versions of the same software elements, possibly with inconsistencies in their design, implementation, and usage. The system will be used in unanticipated ways, giving rise to conditions that were not considered when some of its constituent parts were designed. Changes in usage patterns will stress the system, leading to clashes of assumptions about how long operations take, how much storage is available, or how much data can be processed by a particular algorithm. Different stakeholders will have different expectations of how the system is to perform.

Changing: Parts of the system will always be changing. The operating environments will be changing as failed hardware is replaced, hardware and software are upgraded (and sometimes downgraded), and configurations of components are modified. Many changes in ULS systems will be dynamic to adapt to evolving mission requirements and operating conditions. As a result, the exact ***composition*** of a ULS system cannot be known when it is being designed and may vary from moment to moment.

Among today's assumptions undermined by this characteristic are the following:

- **The effect of a change can be predicted sufficiently well.** When replacing an element, we assume that we understand sufficiently well which characteristics of the element are essential to the adequate functioning of the system and which are inessential. Because of this knowledge, we can make replacements that are not exactly identical (e.g., different vendor, different code, different performance). The scale of a ULS system increases the likelihood that some seemingly inessential difference between the original and the replaced units will, at least occasionally, have significant consequences. The system must be designed to limit the effect of such unexpected consequences, at least when they are considered harmful.
- **Configuration information is accurate and can be tightly controlled.** When considering the effect of changes on a system, today's change processes for smaller systems make the (mostly reasonable) assumption that the configuration of the system is both known and knowable. In ULS systems, configuration information will never be completely accurate, and yet, despite the inaccuracies, changes must be installed effectively.
- **Components and users are fairly homogeneous.** In architecting and implementing today's systems, we begin by believing that we understand the capabilities of users and how they will use the system. In ULS systems, actual usage will drift from what was anticipated not just because of normal human tendencies, but because of the scale and variety of people involved with the system. Today we often start with the premise that we can control the range of hardware and software components that are employed over the life of the system. The scale of ULS systems will make it more difficult to ensure that each element of the system is reasonably up to date in its software versions, hardware capabilities, etc. The system design will have to take into account these kinds of disparities, which are normally not considered today.

2.5 Erosion of the People/System Boundary

People will not just be users of a ULS system: they will be part of its overall behavior. In addition, the boundary between the system and user/developer roles will blur. Just as people who maintain and modify a city sometimes also live within the city, in a ULS system, sometimes a person will act in the role of a traditional user, sometimes in a supporting role as a maintainer of ***system health,*** and sometimes as a change agent adding and repairing the system's functions.

Considering people to be part of the ULS system means that as the system's configuration and computational capabilities change, processes and procedures must be in place to help people understand how to accomplish their

2 Characteristics of ULS Systems

current objectives and become aware of new possibilities. Equally, as the pattern of usage by people changes (for example, if a large number of people attempt some action more or less simultaneously), the system must have procedures in place to adapt to the changed demand. This kind of interplay will be needed because the size of the system and the number of changes will require the provision of methods for adapting quickly to changes in expectations and capabilities, whether these changes are on the people side or the hardware/software side. Increasing reliance on ***machine learning*** for adaptation could be exploited by adversaries. Therefore a ULS system must also be skeptical as it learns how to adapt to new situations.

The ***law of large numbers*** and the size of ULS systems potentially allow for analyses leading to types of improvement and adaptation that are not feasible in smaller systems. For example, with a sufficiently large number of interactions, the system can begin to gather data on observed regularities in people's behavior and begin to build statistically reliable models of what types of services will be required. These opportunities arise from considering people as integral elements of the overall system's behavior. Although the behavior of individuals can be difficult to predict in isolation, the behavior of large groups is more amenable to analysis.

Among today's assumptions undermined by this characteristic are the following:

- **People are just users of the system.** For some aspects of a ULS system, it will be impossible to understand or analyze the effects of the system without giving full consideration to the behavior of people as elements of it. The inclusion of human behavior in the analysis of overall system function is not new, but, in ULS systems, it will become more imperative than for today's systems.
- **The collective behavior of people is not of interest.** When designing and analyzing ULS systems, their scale means that the collective behavior of groups of users and developers will be a significant factor in how the system is used, viewed, and accepted.
- **Social interactions are not relevant.** Today's emphasis in designing information systems is on the technology—how to make the system sufficiently fast, reliable, functional, etc. It is not often the case that a socio-technical perspective is taken. In ULS systems, desirable emergent behaviors will partly be a function of how groups of people make use of the technology and how the technology supports group needs. Failure to take into account the conventions that govern people's behaviors, failure to take into account the benefits and problems associated with the actions of masses of people, and failure to treat people as a part of the system would be a mistake.

2.6 Normal Failures

Because the physical underpinnings of a ULS system will be vast, hardware failures will no longer be an exception. And because software components will be stressed beyond their designed-for capabilities, software may also behave in undesirable ways. Moreover, even when defects are low, frequency of use may result in a continuing, low-level occurrence of failure events somewhere in the system. For example, if a file transfer protocol fails once in a million uses but the transfer protocol is used a million times a day, a failure will occur, on average, once a day. We can expect that, with ULS systems, unusual situations and boundary conditions will occur often enough that something will *always* be failing.

Because of the scale of ULS systems, they must be designed to cope with failures (of various kinds) as a continuous problem. This realization may sound daunting or pessimistic, but we are familiar with this effect in our everyday lives. In a large city, there will be an occasional fire, crime, or accident often enough that it is worth having fire, police, and ambulance services. But the occurrence of fires, crimes, or accidents in any given building is sufficiently rare that we don't have these services for each building. We know that these problems are inevitable, so we can make them a part of the community infrastructure. Similarly, in ULS systems, the types of failures that occur infrequently in smaller scale systems will occur frequently enough that the ULS system will have to support special capabilities for dealing with them on a regular basis. This means not just designing systems to cope with the consequences of such failures, but designing them to contain the effects of failures and, to the extent possible, to give warnings before the failures occur or have a widespread impact.

Among today's assumptions undermined by this characteristic are the following:

- **Failures will occur infrequently.** The scale of ULS systems can increase the number of failures per unit of time—as system usage and size increase, certain types of failure will be "normal." ULS systems must be designed to limit how much of the ULS system's behavior is affected by failure.

- **Defects can be removed.** Much of software engineering is devoted to the prevention and detection of defects; yet in very large systems, it is impossible to be sure that all defects have been removed, and, in practice, more often than not, systems are shipped and used despite the presence of defects. ULS system design must pay more attention to fault tolerance than is typically paid (except for high-assurance systems). In addition, ULS systems, because of their scale, will almost certainly introduce new types of faults that will require new fault-tolerance strategies.

2 Characteristics of ULS Systems

2.7 New Paradigms for Acquisition and Policy

Because of its size, those responsible for making a ULS system possible (managers, acquirers, developers, suppliers, legislators, etc.) will be unable to comprehensively define and control uncertain and ever-changing stakeholder requirements. Any requirement for centralized, global control over changes cannot possibly take all these different purposes into account, manage them efficiently, or allow for rapid changes in response to immediate needs. A successful ULS system must have the ability to develop organically. Our vision is not unbridled anarchy: as in cities, there will be rules, regulations, zoning laws, governing officials, and enforcement personnel to keep things going, allowing citizens to adapt to meet local needs while maintaining a viable overall structure.

The size of ULS systems will present a challenge to managers. If the actual needs of system stakeholders can never be fully anticipated, the entire contracting, design, and construction process—no matter how closely managed for quality control—will all too often result in systems that fail to meet users' expectations and needs.

One of today's assumptions undermined by this characteristic is the following:

A prime contractor is responsible for system development, operation, and evolution. The centralized control implied by the usual prime-contractor model is incompatible with ULS systems. For example, there is no prime contractor in charge of the development, operation, and evolution of the Internet, although there are organizations that have responsibility for some portions of Internet capability. Despite this decentralized approach, the Internet has evolved successfully. Of course, there is a certain amount of centralization with respect to the development and evolution of interface standards, but much of the development, operation, and evolution of Internet services and core capabilities does not follow a prime-contractor model.

2.8 Summary

Although today's systems have some of the characteristics identified in this section, what will distinguish ULS systems is that they will have *all* of these characteristics. Consequently, as we have noted above, many key assumptions we make today will be undermined: these systems will surpass the thresholds at which today's approaches will work even nominally. To understand the challenges posed by ULS systems, we will need to look at them differently, not just as systems or systems of systems, but as ***socio-technical ecosystems:*** *socio-technical* because they are composed of people and technology interacting in complex ways, and *ecosystem* because characterizing them in this way will give us the richest understanding of the technical and management problems that will be encountered when building, operating, and developing them.

3 Challenges In ULS Systems

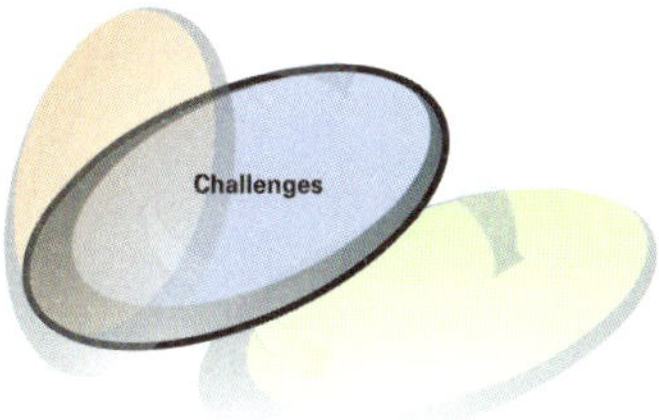

Section 2 described how the characteristics of ULS systems challenge the fundamental assumptions of today's software developers and acquirers. It is clear that today's approaches to defining, developing, deploying, operating, acquiring, and evolving software-intensive systems will not suffice. The success of ULS systems and the achievement of the missions that they are intended to support depend on the development of new capabilities. If we characterize ULS systems as cities or socio-technical ecosystems, we find that current knowledge and practices are geared toward creating individual *buildings* or *species*. What we lack is a scientific understanding of, and adequate methods and technologies for, effectively developing software-intensive systems on the scale of whole *cities* or ***ecosystems***. These gaps in knowledge and capability are strategic, not tactical. They are unlikely to be addressed adequately by incremental research within established categories. Rather, we need to develop a broad new conception of both the nature of such systems and new ideas for how to develop them. Understanding the demands that ULS systems will make is key to defining the research that is needed for new solutions.

The challenges that we will face in developing ULS systems are organized in three broad areas:

1. Design and Evolution
2. Orchestration and Control
3. Monitoring and Assessment

3 Challenges in ULS Systems

3.1 Design and Evolution

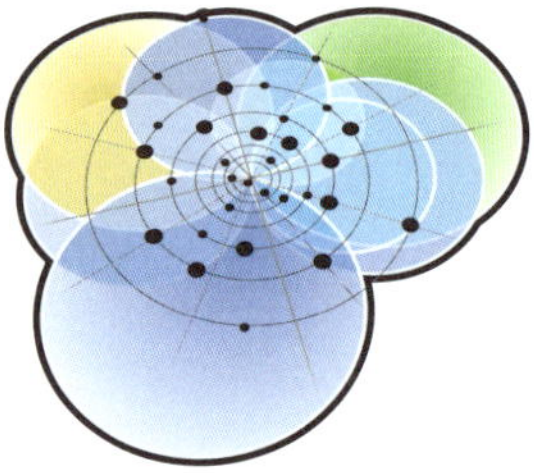

How do we systematically address the socio-technical ecosystem characteristics of ULS systems? How do we design the ecosystem infrastructure, which includes the services provided by and to the participants in the system, the rules (both formal and social) guiding their behavior, the acquisition practices, the supply-chain infrastructure, economic issues, etc.? How do we design the organizational processes responsible for producing and continually updating the designs of ULS system components and integration schemes?

The scale of complexity and uncertainty in ULS system design will be so great as to resist treatment by traditional development methods, which are characterized by centralized control (true even of decentralized methods such as open-source development) and by the testing of a small number of hypotheses about what constitutes a good solution. The challenge will be to find new ways to harness and coordinate the design capabilities and motivations not just of individual companies, prime contractors, and supply chains, but of whole industries, within which competition for value will drive much richer and more economical exploration of complex ***design spaces.*** Developing and evolving architectures around which industries will organize presents challenges that we are not equipped to understand today. Maintaining the conceptual integrity of system designs in the context of such decentralized design activities spread across the economy will present challenges to current knowledge, tools, and methods. The design of the industrial ecosystems, including incentive structures and sources of value (including procurement practices) that drive them, requires new thinking and integrative research across numerous disciplines. We need a new science to support the ***design of all levels*** of the systems that will eventually produce the ULS systems we can envision, but not implement effectively, today.

ULS systems will be deeply embedded in the real world. These systems will comprise not only information technology (IT) components, but also machines of many kinds, individuals and teams, diverse sensors, information streams and stores (including verbal and non-verbal human communications), and so forth. We have traditionally viewed software as programming the *computer* components of such systems. We face a challenge in understanding and designing software in a new way: as the programming of *all* of the information-processing mechanisms and behaviors of complex ULS systems.

The characterization of systems as information-processing mechanisms is not new; it dates back at least to Wiener's concept of ***cybernetics.*** [12] However, recent developments in areas such as computer science and ***distributed cognition*** put us in a position to reconsider how information is processed in truly complex systems and to design their underlying information processes to make them sentient, adaptive, and effective in performing complex missions.

Finally, adding new capabilities to our systems today is a laborious process of redesign and reengineering. ULS systems will require internal infrastructure and mechanisms to facilitate the development and introduction of such improvements whether they are initiated by system designers, implementers, and operators or the users and computational elements interior to the ULS system. New theories of ULS system evolution will help to provide the rules and mechanisms needed to facilitate effective evolution of these systems, but the challenges in accomplishing this exceed our current change-management research and practice.

Listed below is a sample of specific challenges in ULS system design and evolution. Each one can be mapped to the characteristics described in Section 2. For example, *economics and industry structure* deals with how to align the structure of systems with industry elements and economic forces to discover and meet key ULS requirements. This challenge relates to the *decentralization* and *new paradigms for acquisition and policy* characteristics; the issue is how to engage industrial partners in developing and evolving ULS systems when a different acquisition and management control model is needed. It relates to the characteristics of *inherently conflicting, unknowable, and diverse requirements* and *heterogeneous, inconsistent, and changing elements* because these factors affect how the contractual mechanisms will have to work. The *normal failures* characteristic affects the acceptance criteria for contractor work.

- **economics and industry structure:** How do we align ***design architectures***[13] and industry structures to harness economic forces in the service of discovering and meeting key requirements?
- **social activity for constructing computational environments:** How do we model interaction with a social context in a way that offers guidance for how to design and support ULS systems?

12 Norbert Wiener (1894-1964): Wiener's work before and during World War II led to the publishing of *Cybernetics, or Control and Communication in the Animal and Machine* in 1948. In it, he described a new way of looking at how the world functioned based on his research on the way in which information is transmitted and processed. He saw a world that focused on information, not energy and on digital or numeric processes, not machine or analog processes.

13 By *design architecture* we mean a set of decisions that partitions the task of producing the *complete* design for a system into a set of largely separable subtasks.

3 Challenges in ULS Systems

- **legal issues:** How will we resolve the legal issues that would today prevent a ULS system from achieving its full potential? These issues include licensing, intellectual property, and liability concerns that arise due to the size and complexity of a ULS system that is developed under multiple authorities. How will legal policies (e.g., regarding the ***certification*** of security- and safety-critical components) adapt (if at all) to the characteristics of ULS systems (e.g., to self-reconfigurability as a pervasive technical characteristic)?

- **enforcement mechanisms and processes:** How do we create enforcement mechanisms for the set of (legal, design, and process) rules that support and maintain the integrity of the system? What structures are required to negotiate exceptions to the rules so that the ULS system can be adaptable without affecting its long-term sustainment?

- **definition of common services supporting the ULS system:** How do we define an infrastructure (a set of technological, legal, and social services) that will be common to many elements of the ULS system?

- **rules and regulations:** How will whole industries come together to agree on rules and regulations to ensure overall coherence and quality while still being sufficiently flexible to permit stakeholders to explore and compete within rich design spaces?

- **agility:** How can the groups responsible for ULS development, maintenance, and evolution be kept sufficiently agile to respond effectively to changes in requirements, system configuration, system environment, etc.?

- **handling of change:** How can the processes for developing, maintaining, and evolving a ULS system be adapted to handle in situ design change and evolution rather than relying on static requirements preceding design and implementation?

- **integration:** How can we minimize the effort needed to integrate components built independently by different teams, with different goals, and at different times to create the current system?

- **user-controlled evolution:** How do we provide components and composition rules that give users the ability to create new, unplanned capabilities?

- **computer-supported evolution:** How do we provide automated methods to evolve ULS systems?

- **adaptable structure:** How do we create designs that are effective even as requirements and the ULS environment change continually?

- **emergent quality:** How do we organize processes for producing ULS systems so that they converge on high-quality designs?

3.2 Orchestration and Control

By ***orchestration*** we mean the set of activities needed to make the elements of a ULS system work in reasonable harmony to ensure continuous satisfaction of the mission objectives. Orchestration involves management and administration but at a scale well beyond that of traditional, centralized, relatively fine-grained controls. Orchestration requires a combination of up-front design, overall policy promulgation and enforcement, and real-time adjustment of operating parameters.

Orchestrating a ULS system requires supporting interdependencies and controlling the consequences of local actions with respect to their effect on the emergent whole, even though each part of a system might be acting to maximize its local utility. In a city, for example, when different groups want more services than can be provided, there are procedures for deciding what gets provided and to whom. The city governance authorities do not control the actions of individual citizens, but they do specify general rules of behavior that are intended to minimize unnecessary conflict, disruption, or uneconomic use of city resources. Similarly, the policies and inherent capabilities that constrain the interactions of the participants in a ULS ecosystem create a framework for the long-term viability and adaptability of a ULS system in a world of changing missions, deployments, and required functionality.

Orchestration is needed at all levels of ULS systems. At one level, the activities of otherwise autonomous companies developing key technologies for ULS systems will need to be orchestrated. At another level, the behaviors of a ULS system in operation will need to allocate resources in real time to satisfy real-time mission objectives. At the highest level, orchestration could both affect and be driven by doctrine, policy, appropriations, and procurement practices.

This style of system management is fundamentally different from the way we manage systems today. To succeed in developing and operating ULS systems, we thus need new knowledge, technologies, and methods in the following areas:

- **online modification:** How can necessary adjustments to a system be made while the system is running, with minimal disturbance to user services; how can the changes be propagated throughout the system when necessary?
- **maintenance of quality of service:** How can the overall quality of service be maintained while enabling the flexibility to provide different levels of service to different groups?
- **creation and execution of policies and rules:** What policies and rules lead to effective solutions despite divergent viewpoints of stakeholders? How are such rules and policies created? How are they executed?

3 Challenges in ULS Systems

- **adaptation to users and contexts:** How can the needs of users and stakeholders be discovered and understood; how can those needs be translated into execution-time modifications and adaptations? How can the context—both the user's context and the physical context—be sensed, captured, and translated into adaptations?
- **enabling of user-controlled orchestration:** How do we provide components and composition rules that give users the ability to adapt and customize portions of the system in the field?

3.3 Monitoring and Assessment

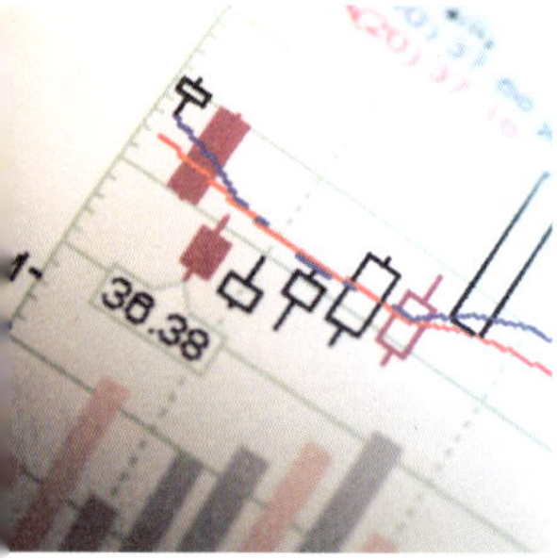

The effectiveness of ULS system design, evolution, and orchestration has to be evaluated. There must be an ability to monitor and assess ULS system state, behavior, and overall health and well being. The monitoring and assessment of complex systems, and subsequent adjustment of system parameters, is not a new idea. In a city, for example, sensors collect information about traffic conditions, and this information is then distributed to those to whom it is relevant, allowing people to select alternate routes around traffic jams, for example. In complex telecommunication, transportation, and electrical distribution networks, continuous measurements are made of system configuration, resource usage and demand, system and component failure status, etc. Measurements are taken by monitoring embedded sensors. Assessment activities then determine what the measurements mean, such as by simulating the future health of the system or determining the need for control or orchestration actions.

The criteria for success or overall health are different for ULS systems than for smaller systems designed to accomplish a task that does not change as the system is used. For example, consider criteria for the success of a city. Different criteria are used by the governing bodies, different groups of citizens, etc. If the power fails in one part of the city, the rest of the city may not be overly inconvenienced, at least as long as the power failure does not last too long, impair some critical facility, or happen too often. Because a city provides distributed services to different groups of people, its success in delivering services will depend in part on the expectations and needs of each group and in part on the qualities of the delivered service. Understanding such criteria is a critical aspect of the monitoring and assessment of a ULS system.

The primary approach today to system monitoring and assessment is through the use of metrics. We characterize the quality or functionality of a system by a set of metrics captured at critical probe points defined for the system's constituent components and networks. This is far from adequate for ULS systems. Our current measurement science is analogous to a small set of tests, each like a specific X-ray or MRI scan for a broken bone, whereas we need ensemble *indicators* of a ULS system's overall health, fitness, and well being.

The scale, decentralization, distribution, and heterogeneity of ULS systems will present challenges to effective monitoring and assessment. Among other things, it is likely that some ULS system indicators should be statistical, composite measures of a system's overall state—akin to the gross domestic product or to measuring climate change by estimates such as the net loss or gain of ice mass. To maintain a ULS system at a set of reasonable expectations, to influence the direction of its evolution, and to assess and predict its overall quality and effective functionality, we will need to augment current measurement approaches with additional new theories and practices. Finally, because ULS systems are socio-technical systems with people as participants, ULS system indicators must reflect the conditions not only of the technological but also the human, organizational, economic, and business elements of the system.

Examples of challenges associated with monitoring and assessment are the following:

- **defining the indicators:** What system-wide, end-to-end, and local quality-of-service indicators are relevant to meeting user needs and ensuring the long-term viability of the ULS system?
- **understanding why indicators change:** What adjustments or changes to system elements and interconnections will improve or degrade these indicators?
- **prioritizing the indicators:** Which indicators should be examined under what conditions? Are indicators ordered by generality, so that some give an overall health reading of the system while others are specialized to particular diagnostics?
- **handling change and imperfect information:** How do the monitoring and assessment processes handle continual changes to components, services, usage, connectivity, etc? Note that imperfect information can be inaccurate, stale, or imprecise.
- **gauging the human elements:** What are the indicators of the health and performance of the people, business, and organizational elements of the ULS system?

4 Overview of Research Areas

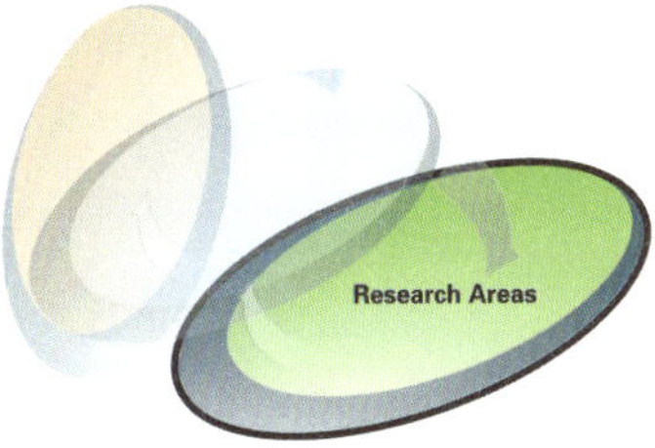

We introduce an interdisciplinary portfolio of seven research areas that address the three challenge categories of ULS system design evolution, orchestration and control, and monitoring and assessment. Because the characteristics of ULS systems fundamentally undermine the assumptions of today's approaches, breakthrough research is necessary in all three areas to meet the current, near-term, and long-term needs of ULS systems. Because of the ecosystem nature of ULS systems, we must take a more expansive view of software research and include its interactions with associated research in the physical and social sciences. The seven research areas are the following:

1. **Human Interaction:** Understanding ULS system behavior will depend on the view that humans are elements of a socially constituted computational process. This research involves anthropologists, sociologists, and social scientists conducting detailed socio-technical analyses of user interactions in the field, with the goal of understanding how to construct and evolve such socio-technical systems effectively.

2. **Computational Emergence:** Some aspects of ULS systems will be "programmed" by properly incentivizing and constraining behavior rather than by explicitly prescribing. This research area explores the use of methods and tools based on economics and ***game theory*** (e.g., ***mechanism design***) to ensure globally optimal ULS system behavior by exploiting the strategic self-interests of the system's constituencies. This research area also includes exploring ***metaheuristics*** and ***digital evolution*** to augment the cognitive limits of human designers, so they can manage ongoing ULS system adaptation more effectively.

4 Overview of Research Areas

3 **Design:** This research area broadens the traditional technology-centric definition of design to include people and organizations; social, cognitive, and economic considerations; and design structures such as ***design rules*** and government policies. It involves research in support of designing ULS systems from all of these points of view and at many levels of ***abstraction***, from the hardware to the software to the people and organizations in which they work.

4 **Computational Engineering:** ULS systems will be defined in many languages, each with its own abstractions and semantic structures. This research area focuses on evolving the expressiveness of representations to accommodate this semantic diversity. Because the complexity of ULS systems will challenge human comprehension, this area also focuses on providing automated support for computing the behavior of components and their compositions in systems and for maintaining desired properties as ULS systems evolve.

5 **Adaptive System Infrastructure:** This research area investigates integrated development environments and runtime ***platforms*** that support the decentralized nature of ULS systems. This research also focuses on technologies, methods, and theories that will enable ULS systems to be developed in their deployment environments.

6 **Adaptable and Predictable System Quality:** Managing traditional qualities such as security, performance, reliability, and usability is necessary but not sufficient to meet the challenges of ULS systems. This research area focuses on how to maintain quality in a ULS system in the face of continuous change, ongoing failures, and attacks. It also includes identifying, predicting, and controlling new indicators of ***system health*** (akin to the U. S. gross domestic product) that are needed because of the scale of ULS systems.

7 **Policy, Acquisition, and Management:** This research area focuses on transforming acquisition policies and processes to accommodate the rapid and continuous evolution of ULS systems by treating suppliers and supply chains as intrinsic and essential components of a ULS system.

While this collection of research areas is not exhaustive, it represents the spectrum of research that is needed for designing, deploying, and managing systems as they evolve toward ultra-large scale. Table 1 shows the relationship between the seven research areas described and the challenges described in Section 3. Meeting these challenges requires a wide spectrum of research in a variety of disciplines beyond computer science and software engineering, an expansion of our computational foundations, and perhaps even new foundations. A dot in the following table indicates that the research area addresses a portion of the indicated challenge.

Table 1: Relationship Between Research Areas and Challenges

Research Areas	Design and Evolution	Orchestration and Control	Monitoring and Assessment
Human Interaction	●	●	
Computational Emergence	●	●	
Design	●		
Computational Engineering	●		
Adaptive System Infrastructure		●	●
Adaptable and Predictable System Quality	●	●	●
Policy, Acquisition, and Management	●	●	

The remainder of this section elaborates on Table 1 by explaining how each research area addresses one or more of the challenges presented in Section 3. Detailed descriptions of the research areas as well as their associated research topics are presented in Part II of this report.

4.1 Human Interaction

Research in the area of **Human Interaction** addresses some of the challenges in **Design and Evolution** and **Orchestration and Control**.

Relevance to Design and Evolution. People are key participants in ULS systems. Many problems in complex systems today stem from failures at the individual and organizational level. We therefore need research on user-centered specifications and on **Modeling Users and User Communities**.[14] At the heart of this research are empirical methods, such as those used in ethnography, sociology, cognitive and brain science, and anthropology.

14 **Bold** formatting indicates that this research topic is described in detail in Part II, Section 6 and referred to in the tables in Section 5.

4 Overview of Research Areas

While some models of human interaction are inspired primarily by economic factors and competitive forces to drive improvements, research is needed to understand other models, such as open source, that involve **Fostering Non-Competitive Social Collaboration.** In these models, pure self-interest is supplanted by altruistic motivations and the desire to be perceived as productive and intelligent. Since ULS systems will outlast specific people and organizations, ULS system **Longevity** requires research in the organizational structures needed to ensure consistency and robustness as management, personnel, and strategies change over time.

Relevance to Orchestration and Control. Research is also needed in ***Context-Aware Assistive Computing*** to model and develop accurate and robust sensing, filtering, aggregation, and visualization capabilities directed at operating ULS systems. These models will help people by significantly reducing inessential distractions and demands on their attention and anticipating their needs while they orchestrate and use ULS systems. Research in these areas also involves **Understanding Users and Their Contexts** to develop models of human expectations in varying contexts and create techniques to represent and automatically adjust those models based on experience.

4.2 Computational Emergence

Research in the area of **Computational Emergence** addresses some of the challenges in **Design and Evolution** and **Orchestration and Control.**

Relevance to Design and Evolution. ULS systems will often lack a central locus of operational or institutional control. They must therefore satisfy the needs of participants at multiple levels of organization (i.e., from individual components and users to whole institutions). It cannot always be assumed that all participants will participate altruistically for the good of the entire system. In many cases, participants will instead behave opportunistically to meet their own mission requirements, irrespective of the goals and objectives of other participants. Economic and game-theoretic ***mechanism designs*** and related approaches may play an important role in achieving globally optimal behavior precisely because they assume the strategic self-interested behavior of key stakeholders and constituencies. **Algorithmic Mechanism Design** puts mechanism design into a computational setting by using computers to design mechanisms and using mechanisms to control computing. As the design challenges of ULS systems exceed the capabilities of human designers, we will increasingly depend on computational support for software and system design in much the same way as we employ model checking and automated layout packages to aid hardware design. While mechanism design is a well-established field in its own right, we need fundamental research to apply the theory to ULS systems (e.g., to steer emergent behavior in desired directions).

While mechanism designs provide optimal solutions at particular instants, they do not address the needs of their users at all times across the lifespan of these systems. Breakthroughs in **Metaheuristics in Software Engineering** and **Digital Evolution** would offer promising means to cope with pressures that inevitably require ULS systems to adapt to new environments and circumstances, including new policies, missions, and mechanisms. Mapping software engineering problems into metaheuristic problems and creating ***objective functions*** and ***mutator functions*** for metaheuristic approaches are research topics in this area. Judiciously used, digital evolution can substantially augment the cognitive limits of human designers and can find novel (possibly counterintuitive) solutions to complex ULS system design problems.

While mechanism designs, digital evolution, and adaptive systems may be constrained to relatively narrow scopes in early phases of ULS systems research, they all enlist the use of computational resources to solve important ULS system-design and evolution challenges. They also highlight a future in which synergy is achieved between digital and human participants in ULS systems.

Relevance to Orchestration and Control. Evolution in ULS systems will rarely occur in discrete, planned steps in a closed environment; instead it will be continuous and dynamic. The rules for continuous evolution must therefore be built into ULS systems and their supporting platforms, processes, and tools so that they will be largely self-reliant and able to cope with dynamically changing environments without constant human intervention. Achieving this goal requires research on ***in situ control, reflection, and adaptation*** to ensure continuous adherence to system functional and quality-of-service policies in the context of rapidly changing operational demands and resource availability.

4.3 Design

Research in the area of **Design** addresses some of the challenges in **Design and Evolution.**

Relevance to Design and Evolution. Fundamental to the design and evolution of ULS systems will be explicit attention to design across logical, spatial, physical, organizational, social, cognitive, economic, and other aspects of the system. Attention to design is also needed across levels of abstraction involving hardware and software and involving procurers, acquirers, producers, integrators, trainers, and users. A key area of research in design is therefore the need for **Design of All Levels** of ULS systems. Research in design includes formulating the architectural designs of ULS systems in terms of **Design Spaces and Design Rules**: design rules that structure design artifacts and design spaces around which decentralized design activities—and even whole industry structures—may come to be organized. Design rules generalize from traditional interface specifications to structure design artifacts using a much broader concept of constraints that serve to regulate decentralized design processes, largely to assure that component parts will integrate into systems having specified properties. We need research on designing, representing, and analyzing design spaces and on the means by which design rules are created, validated, and changed.

The overall design activity—in some cases carried out across entire industry sectors, including open-source projects, university projects, and individual contributions—then acts as a complex adaptive system, strongly driven to converge economically[15] on, and to maintain, good designs. Today we have few tested theories or practices of designing ULS systems for economic value or of how to establish economic forces that promote good design, such as through new contracting and acquisition structures. We therefore need research on **Harnessing Economics to Promote Good Design** leading to a deeper understanding of how to organize designs and design activities to maximize value and on how to create economic conditions that predictably provide incentives to create and sustain valuable designs.

Operational ULS systems will also behave as complex adaptive systems in which feedback and control are essential to meet user and mission objectives. We therefore need research to understand how to decentralize design activities so that they are responsive to feedback from deployed running systems. Since ULS systems will serve different classes of users with distinct and often conflicting interests, research is needed on **Design Representation and Analysis** and reconciliation of distinct and competing interests, both offline and online and at various levels up and down echelons.

Today's large-scale systems are often characterized by attempts to leverage components that were not designed to work together or that are inconsistent with the design rules of the system architecture in which they are inserted. The success of ULS systems will depend on significant progress being made on ULS system **Assimilation**, where nonconformant components (often with less than adequate reliability) are assimilated into architecturally coherent and robust ULS systems. This research will focus on developing techniques that enable analyzing, modeling, fortifying, and evolving large legacy code bases; working with diverse data; and integrating diverse, uncertain, and unreliable information sources into a coherent operational picture.

15 Economic concerns also include the systems of value used by open-source communities, university projects, and individual efforts. These concerns might not all be monetary value systems, but they all result in forces that promote improvement of the designs.

ULS systems will exacerbate today's problems in **Determining and Managing Requirements** due to the scope of application domains that exceed limits of human intellectual capabilities, the complexity and fragmentation of socio-economic processes and organizations that are highly decentralized and autonomous, and the sheer complexity of the problems being addressed. Analysis and design methods must accommodate pervasive incompleteness, imperfection, uncertainty, and nondeterminacy in the products and processes that arise throughout the system's development and evolution. We need research on ULS system-requirements topics, such as the basics of requirements gathering, conflict management, ambiguity tolerance, and requirements phaseout.

4.4 Computational Engineering

Research in the area of **Computational Engineering** addresses some of the challenges in **Design and Evolution.**

Relevance to Design and Evolution. ULS systems will require new approaches to intellectual control for developers and users with different backgrounds and objectives. Research on **Expressive Representation Languages**, more comprehensive programming and abstraction mechanisms, and more powerful capabilities for modularity and composition will be required. In addition, we need new techniques to support the rich semantic web that exists among artifacts that will make up ULS systems, including policies, specifications, designs, implementations, documentation, legacy code, and many others.

Because ULS systems will be highly decentralized, they will depend heavily on trusted core components and standards throughout their architectures. While complete upfront specification of ULS systems will be impractical, an important subset of trusted components and standards will require comprehensive specification to support extremely rigorous ***validation***, ***verification***, and ***certification***. We need research to define ULS-capable **Scaled-Up Specification, Verification, and Certification** technologies. Research is also needed to understand how model-based, aspect-oriented, and other generative methods can help satisfy stringent certifiability and reliability requirements.

The design and construction of ULS systems will benefit from scaling up the granularity of reliable engineering artifacts. A billion-line system becomes a million-unit system if the reliable unit of construction is a component of a thousand lines and becomes a ten-unit or hundred-unit system if hundred-thousand-line or ten-thousand-line subsystems, respectively, can be reliably built from reliable thousand-line components. Fast and correct development of such large components will require automation of the computational analysis and verification of ULS system specifications, architectures, designs, and implementations at a level of precision not possible today. We therefore need research on scientific foundations in support of **Computational Engineering for Analysis and Design** to compute the behavior and ***quality attributes*** defined by programs and their associated specification and design artifacts. This research is also required for automated composition of components in highly decentralized and distributed architectures. In addition, as ULS systems evolve and adapt to changing operating conditions, we must develop methods for automated computation and maintenance of correct definitions of system behavior.

4.5 Adaptive System Infrastructure

Research in the area of **Adaptive System Infrastructure** addresses some of the challenges in **Orchestration and Control** and **Monitoring and Assessment.**

Relevance to Orchestration and Control. Today's software-development and deployment environments are oriented toward traditional software-development practices that produce and execute software artifacts and centralize activities in a single organization or with central points of control, as in traditional prime/subcontractor structures and open-source development. ULS systems, in contrast, face a broader set of issues:

- Development, deployment, and operational activities will be more integrated and overlapping in ULS systems.
- ULS systems will have many concurrent information flows and will be produced by decentralized design processes.
- Deployment environments that span organizational boundaries will require development environments to assure security and privacy.
- Because of the blurring of the distinction between design time and runtime, ULS systems will increasingly be developed in situ.

These characteristics of ULS systems imply the need for research in **Decentralized Production Management,** including

- investigation of multi-team, multi-organization interoperability;
- new approaches to multi-institution security; and
- coordinated system testing throughout all the software life-cycle phases (as opposed to waiting until system integration).

Since ULS systems will increasingly be developed in situ in the deployment environment, research is needed on **Evolutionary Configuration and Deployment,** which entails

- investigating mechanisms for maintaining the desired degree of trustworthiness in deployment configurations when applications use both trusted and untrusted components;
- analyzing the effects of intended changes and propagating changes automatically and robustly into the set of known alternatives without negatively affecting the system's quality of service;
- supporting the coexistence and interoperability between different deployment configurations; and
- automatic rollover to new configurations, monitoring of the operations of these new configurations against expectations, and rollback to proven configurations.

ULS systems will have to respond to emergent behavior on the part of the users and the environments in which the system is situated. As a consequence, ULS systems must be able to observe their own operations, recognize acceptable and unacceptable behaviors, and take corrective action with little or no operator intervention. These adaptations must occur dependably to achieve a balanced level of quality for ULS system participants. Achieving these goals requires research in **In Situ Control and Adaptation,** which focuses on control-theoretic techniques, decentralized resource-management algorithms, predictable reconfiguration, and reflection mechanisms with predictable effects on quality of service and mechanisms for policy-driven configuration migration.

Relevance to Monitoring and Assessment. To enable automated analysis of system properties and synthesis of many implementation details, new tools and platforms are needed to specify modifications at the appropriate level of abstraction. We therefore need research on **View-Based Evolution,** which involves instrumenting the system to update views automatically, navigating among views, controlling execution instrumentation and monitoring, and combining human state with computational state.

4 Overview of Research Areas

4.6 Adaptable and Predictable System Quality

Research in the area of **Adaptable and Predictable System Quality** addresses some of the challenges in **Orchestration and Control**, **Monitoring and Assessment**, and **Design and Evolution**.

Relevance to Orchestration and Control. ULS systems will be long running and must operate robustly in environments fraught with failures, overloads, and attacks. Moreover, ULS systems must maintain robustness in the presence of adaptations that are not centrally controlled or authorized, and which in some cases may be initiated by the systems themselves rather than by human operators. Research is needed to develop theories of **Robustness, Adaptation, and Quality Attributes**, along with supporting mechanisms that accommodate both the traditional concepts of instantaneous robustness and the time-sequenced concept of robustness that arises from the decentralized, adaptive, and long-lived nature of ULS systems. This research includes seeking to uncover signals in development processes (e.g., numbers of reported adaptations) and runtime processes (e.g., system dynamics) that predict impending points of instability and studying robustness mechanisms arising in naturally robust systems.

Some degree of system failures (hardware and software) will be intrinsic to ULS systems. For example, at any given moment, some portion of the Internet is in failure mode. It is inevitable that ULS systems will be tempting targets of attack for capable and motivated adversaries seeking tactical and strategic advantages. We have difficulty achieving high levels of security even for the state-of-the-art systems of systems today. To ensure acceptably high, measurable levels of **Security, Trust, and Resiliency** for ULS systems, research is required in the following topics: security, trust, and resiliency measures and metrics; attack detection; attack containment; graceful degradation under attack; recovery from attacks; and attack diagnostics and forensics.

Engineering Management at Ultra-Large Scales is another topic that must be addressed for ULS systems. Developing practices that foster continuous product and process improvement across organizational boundaries is just one of many issues confronting engineering management at ultra-large scales. Moreover, new product and process measures and new technical infrastructures will be required to support management decision making. Research is needed on how to motivate and manage ULS system knowledge workers and how to develop measurements of system and process, product, and project health.

Relevance to Monitoring and Assessment. In addition to defining entirely new quality attributes, there will also be changes in the way developers and operators of ULS systems specify, analyze, and control quality attributes. Increasing scale requires increasing aggregation and abstraction, which in turn suggests increasing reliance on ***stochastic*** theories of behavior and the need to understand how theories at different levels of abstraction interact with one another. For example, ***Internet storms*** arise at the massive scale of the Internet but do not appear in smaller scale settings. Predicting and averting these types of phenomena require novel theories and applications of approaches inspired by such fields as ***statistical mechanics*** and ***possibility theory***. In general, research on **Scale and Composition of Quality Attributes** is needed to identify new measures; complementary stochastic and ***deterministic*** theories of quality; and verification techniques that accommodate uncertainty arising from ***non determinism***, measurement error, and lack of knowledge.

Relevance to Design and Evolution. Predicting and preserving system-wide qualities require establishing and sustaining the system invariants on which these qualities depend. A variety of enforcement mechanisms have been developed over many years of practice—transaction monitors, security monitors, sandboxes, and schedulers, to name a few. In some cases, we need new research on scaling these mechanisms to ULS system scale; in other cases, completely new mechanisms are needed. In all cases, the enforcement mechanisms must be linked explicitly with the complementary quality theories. Topics of particular research interest for **Enforcing Quality Requirements** include enforcement mechanisms for shared resources and robust recovery mechanisms and mechanisms for ensuring acceptable levels of computing when operating in suboptimal conditions.

People will be a key part of a ULS system, and the overall quality attributes of the system include quality attributes of humans as well as the technology and the interactions between the two. We therefore need research on **Understanding People-Centric Quality Attributes,** which includes trustworthy human-comprehensible models of system state; modeling human-human interactions, human quality attributes, and crowd behavior; and blending human and system quality attributes.

4 Overview of Research Areas

4.7 Policy, Acquisition, and Management

Research in the area of **Policy, Acquisition, and Management** addresses some of the challenges in **Design and Evolution** and **Orchestration and Control.**

Relevance to Design and Evolution. Just as computational elements of a ULS system will be interdependent, so too will human elements. Not only will the actions of human participants affect other users, but successful operation may depend on appropriate action by other users. The systems must be explicitly designed to accommodate change at all levels, and consequently their acquisition processes must be designed to support dynamic changes in system capabilities. Organizational, technical, and operational policies must be developed and largely automated to enable fast and effective local actions while preserving global capabilities.

Given the scope and scale of ULS systems, technical, organizational, and operational policies will emerge as principal vehicles for ensuring harmonious operations. Therefore **Policy Definition for ULS Systems** must support both local and global operations in such a way that people and the computational actions they initiate can achieve cooperative and even competing objectives without impairing the viability of the system as a whole. Such considerations require definition of policies whose effect on system operations, stability, and long-term viability is well-defined and widely understood. Research is needed in policy definition that allows for flexible collaboration, effective governance and local adaptation, and automated support for making and assessing policy decisions.

Relevance to Orchestration and Control. Given their pervasive application to support global operations in many simultaneous strategic and tactical situations, **Fast Acquisition for ULS Systems** will be required to meet changing threats and environments. Research will be needed in developing new acquisition processes for fast response, integrating supply chains for operational readiness, capitalizing on ad hoc acquisition, and automating for fast acquisition.

Since ULS systems will be designed to support dynamic coalitions and management of tactical and strategic operations in a highly distributed setting, decentralized **Management of ULS Systems** within an overall policy framework will be critical. Research is required in managing ULS systems for operational readiness and organizing supply chains of vendors and integrators for fast system evolution.

5 Summary and Recommendations

The research areas introduced in Section 4 provide an initial research agenda for ULS systems based on the results of our one-year study. Our experience from this study underscored the need for fundamental research breakthroughs across multiple, multi-disciplinary areas in order to solve ULS system challenges. We therefore intend that research and development (R&D) communities be active on numerous fronts. We also intend that as R&D communities increasingly understand the nature of ULS systems, they will identify promising research in areas and topics that are not covered in this report.

Moreover, we have purposely avoided couching our descriptions in terms of today's technology. We are focused on systems of the future, namely ULS systems. The research that will lead us to that future is long term and fundamental. We are aware that some of today's successful software technologies and methodologies are perceived as panaceas for future DoD system development, such as the following:

- ***service-oriented architecture*** (SOA) platforms (such as web services, ***.NET***, ***Enterprise JavaBeans***, and ***CORBA***), which have introduced advanced capabilities to the mainstream IT community and which incorporate various levels of ***middleware*** as part of the overall development process
- the World Wide Web Consortium (WC3), where information-management standards have enabled us to connect independently developed browsers and web pages easily
- ***model-driven architecture*** (MDA), which defines an approach to software development that separates the specification of system functionality from the specification of its implementation on specific platforms by structuring specifications expressed as high-level models rather than platform-specific code
- the High-Performance Computing (HPC) Grid, which is enabling scientists and researchers to collaborate on grand challenge problems such as global climate change modeling and high-energy physics experiments

5 Summary and Recommendations

- the Global Command and Control System (GCCS), which integrated a series of commercially available products into a defined standard suite to provide interoperability among a variety of services and functions in the DoD
- the Global Information Grid (GIG), a net-centric system operating in a global context expected to provide processing, storage, management, and transport of information to support all DoD, national-security, and related intelligence-community missions and functions

These technologies and methodologies and others not cited herald technical progress and will undoubtedly have some bearing on success with ULS systems. In key ways, however, each is deficient in meeting the challenges associated with ULS systems of the future. None addresses the set of root characteristics of ULS systems or the complexity stemming from the scale and the ecosystem nature of ULS systems. Dealing with these characteristics, challenges, and complexity at the fidelity needed for ULS systems requires a new generation of research areas that are informed by—but not necessarily constrained by—the existing technology base.

5.1 Toward a Roadmap for a ULS Systems Research Program

Though our catalog of research areas and topics is a solid beginning, it is insufficient to structure a dedicated research program for ULS systems. Given the scope of the ULS systems problem space, there are many possible approaches to structuring a research program. Since different agencies and organizations have different missions and needs, no single research program is likely to be suitable for all sponsors. As a result, we do not present or prescribe a single roadmap, but instead offer three structures[16] that suggest ways to cluster and prioritize groups of research areas. These structures can then be used to define one or more roadmaps that could lay out one or more ULS systems research programs or projects.

The first structure, described in Sections 5.1.1 and 5.1.2 and summarized in Table 2, maps specific DoD missions and required capabilities to the ULS system research areas and topics in which research is needed to enable achievement of the missions and delivery of the capabilities. The second structure, described in Section 5.1.3 and summarized in Table 3, maps our research areas and topics to the DoD research funding types required to support them. The third structure, presented in Section 5.1.4 and summarized in Table 4, estimates the associated risks and rewards of the research topics in each of the identified research areas.

16 We have defined these structures as illustrated in Tables 2, 3, and 4 to the best of our current understanding. Our categorization of research topics according to mission/capabilities (Table 2), research-funding types (Table 3), and associated risks and rewards (Table 4) is admittedly subjective and is intended as a starting position.

5.1.1 DoD Missions and Capabilities

To tie the research areas to specific DoD capabilities, the following three important missions have been extracted from the 2006 DoD Quadrennial Defense Review (QDR):[17]

Mission 1: Information management of net-centric tactical operations

Mission 2: Tailored, flexible forces

Mission 3: Leverage information technology and innovative concepts to develop interoperable joint C4ISR

Although software was not singled out as an explicit challenge area in the QDR, these three missions rely heavily on software systems that are much larger, more sophisticated, and more complex than those currently available—systems that match the characteristics of ULS systems as we have described them. Below, we describe the goals of each mission and present a pair of associated and required capabilities. These capabilities directly establish the need for breakthroughs and innovations in the research areas that we have identified. For each capability, we then construct a *research track* consisting of the set of pertinent research topics. The research topics are designated by number as they appear in Part II, Section 6 of this report. Those topics in **bold** constitute research that is essential to achieving the capability, while those in plain text will provide support in achieving that capability. All of this information is summarized in Table 2. Our association, though admittedly subjective, forms an initial basis for structuring ULS system research roadmaps.

Mission 1

Mission 1: Information management of net-centric tactical operations. This mission focuses on using connectivity to help joint forces gain greater situational awareness to attack the enemy and avoid fratricide. The QDR illustrates how important it has become to build our joint DoD systems of the future to assure information dominance over all adversaries, conventional nation states, and asymmetric group threats:

> *Achieving the full potential of net-centricity requires viewing information as an enterprise asset to be shared and as a weapon system to be protected. As an enterprise asset, the collection and dissemination of information should be managed by portfolios of capabilities that cut across legacy stove-piped systems. These capability portfolios would include network-based command and control, communications on the move and information fusion. Current and evolving threats highlight the need to design, operate and defend the network to ensure continuity of joint operations. [QDR, page 58]*

17 *Quadrennial Defense Review Report,* February 2006, http://www.defenselink.mil/qdr/report/Report20060203.pdf

5 Summary and Recommendations

Tactical operational systems designed to support the warfighter anywhere and anytime against any adversary must include capabilities that provide timely information to all levels of the theater during tactical operations. Below, we describe two important required capabilities for information management of net-centric tactical operations, along with the research tracks needed to technically enable these capabilities.

- **Capability 1 (C1): Maintain coherent common operating picture by rapidly collecting, processing, disseminating, and protecting information spanning echelons, services, and coalitions across a mix of ultra-large-scale environments.** The needed information will come from an expanding set of information sources, some operated by the DoD, some by our coalition partners, and others in the private sector. Without a capability to manage this information and present a coherent, common, timely, and reliable operating picture to warfighters, we risk either information overload during critical decision-making processes or missing information resulting in wrong decisions.

Research track 1 (RT1):

Essential	Support
M1 (RT1)	M1 (RT1)
6.1.1, 6.1.4, 6.2.1, 6.4.3, 6.5.1, 6.5.3, 6.5.4, 6.6.3, 6.6.4, 6.7.3	6.1.2, 6.1.3, 6.3.3, 6.3.5, 6.6.1, 6.6.5, 6.7.2

- **Capability 2 (C2): Assure ULS system operation in the presence of attack and conduct effective information operations, while denying these capabilities to adversaries.** In addition to getting the right information at the right time to warfighters, we must also prepare for adversaries who will use our reliance on technology to deny our use of that technology in tactical operations. Our ULS systems must therefore incorporate capabilities to assure that they continue to operate while under assault by our adversaries. Likewise, to maintain information dominance during all phases of an operation, our ULS systems must deny the information critical to our adversaries.

Research track 2 (RT2):

Essential	Support
M1 (RT2)	M1 (RT2)
6.1.4, 6.1.5, 6.3.6, 6.4.2, 6.5.4, 6.6.1, 6.6.3, 6.6.4, 6.6.5, 6.7.2	6.1.2, 6.1.3, 6.3.2, 6.3.3, 6.3.4, 6.5.2, 6.6.6, 6.7.1

Mission 2

Mission 2: Tailored, flexible forces. The focus of this mission is on rapid joint mobility and effects-based operations. The QDR articulates the need for a future force that can adapt quickly to changing conditions, incorporate new technology and functions without halting a mission, and smoothly integrate these changes and adaptations without losing any of the previous gains in quality of service or operational capabilities:

> *Rapid global mobility is central to the effectiveness of the future force. The joint force will balance speed of deployment with desired warfighter effects to deliver the right capabilities at the right time and at the right place. Effectiveness of mobility forces will be measured not only by the quantity of material they move, but also by the operational effects they help to achieve. Mobility capabilities will be fully integrated across geographic theaters and between warfighting components and force providers, with response times measured in hours and days rather than weeks. They will enable the Department's move from a large institutional force to a future force that concentrates more operational capabilities at the front line. They will underpin the transition from a Cold War-era garrisoned force to a future force that is tailored for expeditionary operations. [QDR, page 53]*

Future ULS systems that support DoD operations must be as flexible as the forces they support. This flexibility must go beyond current system configuration capabilities to an integrated and continuous improvement capability that rolls out new technology and system capabilities when and as they are needed by commanders and planners. The capabilities required for this mission and their respective research tracks are described below.

- **Capability 3 (C3): Support seamless ULS system operation by rapidly fielding new capabilities in response to new needs and customized deployment environments.** This capability requires an entirely new approach to systems acquisition that can support dynamic changes to operational systems at an ultra-large scale without replacing the system. The ability to field new functions properly is the subject of this capability and research track. Only through a thoroughly different approach will we achieve systems that will support the mobility vision in the QDR.

Research track 3 (RT3):

Essential **(M2) (RT3)**	Support (M2) (RT3)
6.1.5, 6.2.1, 6.2.3, 6.3.1, 6.3.2, 6.3.3, 6.3.5, 6.3.6, 6.4.1, 6.4.3, 6.5.2, 6.5.3, 6.6.6, 6.7.3	6.1.2, 6.4.2, 6.6.3, 6.6.4,

5 Summary and Recommendations

- **Capability 4 (C4): Dynamic adaptation of a ULS system to ensure mission success in a rapidly changing environment.** This capability requires rapid adaptation of a ULS system to a rapidly changing environment. Whether it is deploying to a new theater with entirely different characteristics under carefully planned circumstances or adapting to a surprising new adversarial tactic, the ULS system must support dynamic adaptation that aligns the systems and their functions with the current needs of warfighters in the environment. While this is a manually intensive process today, the future ULS system should automatically adapt to a changing environment, providing warfighters with the necessary information, services, and actions to carry out any mission, anytime, anywhere.

Research track 4 (RT4):

Essential	Support
M2 (RT4)	M2 (RT4)
6.1.1, 6.2.1, 6.2.2, 6.2.3, 6.3.2, 6.3.5, 6.4.2, 6.4.3, 6.5.2, 6.5.3, 6.5.4, 6.6.1, 6.6.5, 6.6.6	6.1.4, 6.1.5, 6.3.3, 6.3.4, 6.6.4

Mission 3

3

Mission 3: Leverage information technology and innovative concepts to develop interoperable joint Command Control Communications Intelligence Surveillance, and Reconnaissance (C4ISR). The focus of this mission is on supporting the global war on terrorism. At its center is a requirement for the global coordination of information from widely diverse sensors to an equally wide variety of analysts' workstations. Both the sensors and analysts will be geographically and politically distributed around the globe, yet must all be coordinated and cooperative. Unlike our current Internet systems, the security requirements and differing policies on information sharing will need a system that can understand and resolve the complex landscape of information-sharing constraints while enabling all of the information sharing that is possible. Current software approaches are adequate for a limited and fixed set of sensors, but are inadequate for the many-to-many information systems that will be needed to support this C4ISR mission as described below by the QDR:

> *The ability of the future force to establish an "unblinking eye" over the battle-space through persistent surveillance will be key to conducting effective joint operations. Future capabilities in ISR, including those operating in space, will support operations against any target, day or night, in any weather, and in denied or contested areas. The aim is to integrate global awareness with local precision. Intelligence functions will be fully integrated with operations down to the tactical level, with far greater ability to reach back to intelligence collection systems and analytic capabilities outside the theater. Supporting this vision will require an architecture that moves intelligence data collected in the theater to the users, rather than*

deploying users to the theater. Future ISR capabilities will be designed to collect information that will help decision-makers mitigate surprise and anticipate potential adversaries' actions. An essential part of the future ISR architecture is a robust missile warning capability. [QDR, page 55]

The joint force of the future will have more robust and coherent joint command and control capabilities. Rapidly deployable, standing joint task force headquarters will be available to the Combatant Commanders in greater numbers to meet the range of potential contingencies. These headquarters will enable the real-time synthesis of operations and intelligence functions and processes, increasing joint force adaptability and speed of action. The joint headquarters will have better information, processes and tools to design and conduct network-enabled operations with other agencies and with international partners. Implementation of Adaptive Planning in the Department will further enhance the lethality of both subordinate standing joint task force headquarters and their parent Combatant Commands by enabling them to produce high-quality, relevant plans in as little as six months. Adaptive Planning is the catalyst that will transform the Department's operational planning processes and systems. Furthermore, Global Force Management, the Department's model for force management, reporting and analysis, will provide Commanders with an unprecedented depth of up-to-date and decision-quality information on unit readiness, personnel and equipment availability. [QDR, page 59]

Unlike the Cold War or any previous military engagements, meeting future DoD operations will require ULS systems to integrate information from everywhere around the globe. In particular, this mission requires systems of the future to fuse, compute, relay, store, and display significantly more information than ever before. The capabilities indicated by this mission are described below, along with their respective research tracks.

- **Capability 5 (C5): Transparent, effective, and secure use of information across commands, allies, and private industry to achieve unity of effort.** This defense capability in turn requires a software capability to manage data on an ultra-large scale as well as to provide information to every participant according to their legitimate access rights, while assuring that the same data cannot be stolen or modified by an adversary.

Research track 5 (RT5):

Essential **M3 (RT5)**	Support M3 (RT5)
6.1.1, 6.1.2, 6.2.1, 6.2.2, 6.3.1, 6.3.6, 6.4.1, 6.4.2, 6.4.3, 6.5.1, 6.6.3, 6.6.5, 6.7.1, 6.7.2	6.1.4, 6.2.3, 6.3.2, 6.3.4, 6.3.5, 6.5.3, 6.6.1, 6.6.6

- **Capability 6 (C6): Application of local context to global information sources to ensure use of the right data anytime, anyplace, for any mission.** The local context can greatly change the interpretation of information. In addition to simply moving the data to the right place at the right time, the ULS system must have the technical capability to turn received information into knowledge that leads to action—by integrating all available data and local context to provide a view that each local user can act upon according to his or her role and access.

Research track 6 (RT6):

Essential (M3) **(RT6)**	Support (M3) (RT6)
6.1.1, 6.1.2, 6.1.3, 6.1.4, 6.1.5, 6.2.1, 6.2.3, 6.3.1, 6.3.2, 6.3.4, 6.3.5, 6.4.1, 6.5.1, 6.5.4, 6.6.2, 6.6.4, 6.7.1, 6.7.3	6.3.3, 6.5.2, 6.6.3, 6.6.5

5.1.2 Research Tracks Associated with Missions and Capabilities

Table 2 illustrates the research tracks RT1–RT6 by summarizing the topics associated with each research area and mapping each to the related missions and capabilities (denoted C1–C6) described above. A full circle ● indicates that the research is necessary to provide this capability (corresponding to the bold numbers in the research tracks), while a half circle ◒ indicates that the research will provide important support for developing the capability (corresponding to the plain-text numbers in the research tracks).

Columns C1/RT1 through C6/RT6 represent research tracks that are necessary (but possibly not sufficient[18]) to achieve the capability indicated. Some topics span a number of research tracks. This crosscutting indicates that results from such topics support multiple capabilities; we advocate an integrated approach to using those results across multiple tracks.

Table 2 can be used to identify and establish priorities for specific research projects either by mission, individual capability, or research topic. These multiple dimensions reflect the various goals and interests of different agencies and individual program managers. They also directly demonstrate the contribution of the research topics to DoD stakeholders.

18 The research track as described lists the research topics deemed essential by the authors of this report. As a particular research track is executed, results of early research in the track may indicate other research that would be necessary to achieve the intended outcome.

Table 2: Research Topics Needed for Specific DoD Missions and Related Capabilities

Research Areas and Topics	Mission 1		Mission 2		Mission 3	
	C1 RT1	C2 RT2	C3 RT3	C4 RT4	C5 RT5	C6 RT6
Human Interaction						
6.1.1 Context-Aware Assistive Computing	●			●	●	●
6.1.2 Understanding Users and Their Contexts	◒	◒	◒		●	●
6.1.3 Modeling Users and User Communities	◒	◒				●
6.1.4 Fostering Non-Competitive Social Collaboration	●	●		◒	◒	●
6.1.5 Longevity		●	●	◒		●
Computational Emergence						
6.2.1 Algorithmic Mechanism Design	●		●	●	●	●
6.2.2 Metaheuristics in Software Engineering				●	●	
6.2.3 Digital Evolution			●	●	◒	●
Design						
6.3.1 Design of All Levels			●		●	●
6.3.2 Design Spaces and Design Rules		◒	●	●	◒	●
6.3.3 Harnessing Economics to Promote Good Design	◒	◒	●	◒		◒
6.3.4 Design Representation and Analysis		◒		◒	◒	●
6.3.5 Assimilation	◒		●	●	◒	●
6.3.6 Determining and Managing Requirements		●	●		●	
Computational Engineering						
6.4.1 Expressive Representation Languages			●		●	●
6.4.2 Scaled-Up Specification, Verification, and Certification		●	◒	●	●	
6.4.3 Computational Engineering for Analysis and Design	●		●	●	●	
Adaptive System Infrastructure						
6.5.1 Decentralized Production Management	●				●	●
6.5.2 View-Based Evolution		◒	●	●		◒
6.5.3 Evolutionary Configuration and Deployment	●		●	●	◒	
6.5.4 In Situ Control and Adaptation	●	●		●		●
Adaptable and Predictable System Quality						
6.6.1 Robustness, Adaptation, and Quality Attributes	◒	●		●	◒	
6.6.2 Scale and Composition of Quality Attributes						●
6.6.3 Understanding People-Centric Quality Attributes	●	●	◒		●	◒
6.6.4 Enforcing Quality Requirements	●	●	◒	◒		●
6.6.5 Security, Trust, and Resiliency	◒	●		●	●	◒
6.6.6 Engineering Management at Ultra-Large Scales		◒	●	●	◒	
Policy, Acquisition, and Management						
6.7.1 Policy Definition for ULS Systems		◒			●	●
6.7.2 Fast Acquisition for ULS Systems	◒	●			●	
6.7.3 Management of ULS Systems	●		●			●

5.1.3 Research Areas by Funding Types

Table 3 groups the seven research areas and topics according to their need for funding at the 6.1 (basic research), 6.2 (applied research), or 6.3 (advanced technology development) levels.[19] In many cases, the areas are sufficiently rich to contain subareas that are at different states of readiness and thus could benefit from multiple levels of funding. In addition, there are other R&D programs under development, such as the Office of the Secretary of Defense's (OSD's) Software-Intensive Systems Producibility Initiative, that will greatly benefit from the 6.1 and 6.2 research of a ULS Systems Research Program, which in turn could reduce the need for extensive 6.3 funding in these programs. The infrastructure to produce experiments and demonstrations of research results can be funded through existing systems-of-systems acquisitions. In turn, these activities will be leveraged by the 6.2 research of a ULS Systems Research Program to produce more rigorous and substantial demonstrations of systems at the scale required to take the results out of laboratory settings to a realistically large and complex DoD environment.

19 For a description of research funding levels, see http://www.cnsronline.org/dodsntfaq.php.

Table 3: Research Topics Categorized by DoD Research Funding Type

Research Areas and Topics	Research Level		
	6.1	6.2	6.3
Human Interaction			
6.1.1 Context-Aware Assistive Computing	●	●	
6.1.2 Understanding Users and Their Contexts	●		
6.1.3 Modeling Users and User Communities	●		
6.1.4 Fostering Non-Competitive Social Collaboration	●		
6.1.5 Longevity	●	●	
Computational Emergence			
6.2.1 Algorithmic Mechanism Design	●		
6.2.2 Metaheuristics in Software Engineering	●		
6.2.3 Digital Evolution	●	●	
Design			
6.3.1 Design of All Levels	●		
6.3.2 Design Spaces and Design Rules	●		
6.3.3 Harnessing Economics to Promote Good Design	●		
6.3.4 Design Representation and Analysis	●	●	
6.3.5 Assimilation	●		
6.3.6 Determining and Managing Requirements	●		
Computational Engineering			
6.4.1 Expressive Representation Languages	●	●	●
6.4.2 Scaled-Up Specification, Verification, and Certification	●	●	
6.4.3 Computational Engineering for Analysis and Design	●	●	
Adaptive System Infrastructure			
6.5.1 Decentralized Production Management	●		
6.5.2 View-Based Evolution	●		
6.5.3 Evolutionary Configuration and Deployment	●	●	●
6.5.4 In Situ Control and Adaptation	●	●	
Adaptable and Predictable System Quality			
6.6.1 Robustness, Adaptation, and Quality Attributes	●	●	
6.6.2 Scale and Composition of Quality Attributes	●		
6.6.3 Understanding People-Centric Quality Attributes	●	●	
6.6.4 Enforcing Quality Requirements	●	●	
6.6.5 Security, Trust, and Resiliency	●	●	
6.6.6 Engineering Management at Ultra-Large Scales	●		
Policy, Acquisition, and Management			
6.7.1 Policy Definition for ULS Systems	●		
6.7.2 Fast Acquisition for ULS Systems	●		
6.7.3 Management of ULS Systems	●		

5 Summary and Recommendations

5.1.4 Research Risk/Reward

The research agenda we are proposing is a mixture of research that builds on some existing groundwork, research that breaks new ground in established areas, and research that is in an entirely new direction. Table 4 provides an initial characterization of the primary topics in each of the seven research areas. As is the purpose of the other tables in this section, Table 4 is intended to help structure a ULS system research project or program by indicating the range of research risk/reward that we are proposing. It can also serve as a companion to Part II, in which we discuss the research details.

Each row in the table is a research area or topic in our proposed agenda. The first column gives the name, and the remaining three columns indicate whether the area already has existing groundwork, whether it is breaking ground in an established area, or whether it represents a new direction. These three categories are not mutually exclusive. We use a blank plus two marks to indicate three levels: a blank cell means that we are not proposing work in this category; a half circle ◒ in a cell means that we are proposing some new work; and a full circle ● in a cell means that we are proposing substantial new work. The marks in this table are substantiated by the detailed descriptions of the research areas and topics found in Section 6.

Table 4: Research Areas and Range of Risk/Reward

Research Areas and Topics	Existing Groundwork	Breaking Ground	New Direction
Human Interaction			
6.1.1 Context-Aware Assistive Computing	●		
6.1.2 Understanding Users and Their Contexts	●	●	
6.1.3 Modeling Users and User Communities		◒	●
6.1.4 Fostering Non-Competitive Social Collaboration		●	◒
6.1.5 Longevity	●	◒	◒
Computational Emergence			
6.2.1 Algorithmic Mechanism Design	●	◒	●
6.2.2 Metaheuristics in Software Engineering	●	◒	
6.2.3 Digital Evolution	●	◒	
Design			
6.3.1 Design of All Levels	●	●	◒
6.3.2 Design Spaces and Design Rules		●	●
6.3.3 Harnessing Economics to Promote Good Design	●	●	●
6.3.4 Design Representation and Analysis		●	◒
6.3.5 Assimilation	●	●	●
6.3.6 Determining and Managing Requirements	●	●	◒
Computational Engineering			
6.4.1 Expressive Representation Languages	◒	●	●
6.4.2 Scaled-Up Specification, Verification, and Certification	◒	●	
6.4.3 Computational Engineering for Analysis and Design	◒	●	●
Adaptive System Infrastructure			
6.5.1 Decentralized Production Management		◒	●
6.5.2 View-Based Evolution	◒	●	●
6.5.3 Evolutionary Configuration and Deployment	●	◒	◒
6.5.4 In Situ Control and Adaptation	●	●	◒
Adaptable and Predictable System Quality			
6.6.1 Robustness, Adaptation, and Quality Attributes		●	●
6.6.2 Scale and Composition of Quality Attributes	◒	●	◒
6.6.3 Understanding People-Centric Quality Attributes	◒	●	●
6.6.4 Enforcing Quality Requirements	◒	●	
6.6.5 Security, Trust, and Resiliency		●	
6.6.6 Engineering Management at Ultra-Large Scales	◒		●
Policy, Acquisition, and Management			
6.7.1 Policy Definition for ULS Systems	◒	●	
6.7.2 Fast Acquisition for ULS Systems	◒	●	●
6.7.3 Management of ULS Systems	◒	●	

5 Summary and Recommendations

5.2 Recommendations

The goal of the above three structures is to both justify and support the development of a plan for a substantive, long-term, funded ULS System Research Program—a program that will marshal the talent of researchers who are experts in the diverse set of disciplines needed to conduct the proposed research. Although it is premature to prescribe a definitive roadmap for ULS system research, Tables 2–4 suggest possible ways to set priorities. We expect that sponsors with different needs will likely choose to support different combinations of research and perhaps different paths through (or projects within) the research program.

As a first step, we recommend the funding and establishment of a ULS System Research Startup Initiative, which would consist of a subset of the contributors to this report as well as other experts with a history of success in the proposed research areas. Over the course of the next two years, this initiative will take the following actions:

- Begin to work with others in the community to conduct new basic research in the areas of **Human Interaction**, **Computational Emergence**, and **Design**. Work in the other areas should follow as soon thereafter as practical.
- Build on existing research efforts and capabilities in the identified research areas to apply them to ULS system challenges.
- Take the ULS system research agenda to a greater level of fidelity and develop a definitive roadmap based on the objectives of the key sponsors.
- Foster the growth of a community of informed stakeholders and researchers.
- Formulate and issue an initial Broad Agency Announcement (BAA) to attract researchers with proven expertise in the diverse set of disciplines (e.g., software engineering, economics, human factors, cognitive psychology, sociology, systems engineering, and business policy) that are collectively required to conduct the proposed research.

As a result of this study, a community of interest in ULS systems and the needed research is already beginning to grow. Contributors to this study have begun to describe and advocate ULS system challenges and potential research. Over the course of the past year, keynote presentations and invited talks related to this study have been given at a diverse set of forums. Workshops and panel discussions are being organized, and the term "ultra-large-scale systems" is gaining traction with others outside the original group charged to conduct the study. As others in the research community become familiar with the ULS system characteristics and challenges, we expect that new research topics and research areas will be proposed. We welcome the community's ideas and contributions.

5.3 Study Conclusion

We have described the characteristics of ULS systems, the associated technical challenges, and the need for a bold, new perspective. We have defined promising research areas and structures that can bolster the definition of a ULS System Research Program. After one year of study, we are certain that new long-term research is required to fulfill the DoD's vision of the future.

The challenges described in this report are not science fiction; they are coming, and much more rapidly than this report's research-oriented charter might suggest. The Internet is a precursor ULS system that is already in widespread use, and the U. S. power, communication, and transport grids currently exhibit many ULS characteristics. Other such systems will doubtless follow.

The fact that the worldwide Internet was constructed without any massive research and development program might suggest that future systems will be produced with similar ease. The problem, however, is that, with the current state of software technology and practice, such systems cannot be built to accomplish specific objectives—much less future DoD missions—on predictable schedules or for affordable budgets. To have any chance of meeting the future needs for such systems, a research program like that described in this report must be initiated now.

It is no exaggeration to say that the operational capabilities of the DoD will increasingly depend on software capabilities equal to the challenges of ULS systems. Software capability cannot be taken for granted in the DoD vision of the future. In the absence of new scientific knowledge and engineering know-how, were a ULS system needed to meet a perceived need, it would now have to be designed and built with current software technology and the traditional acquisition-and-contracting model. While these may be the best-known approaches, they have consistently been proven inadequate.

The proposed ULS system research is broader and deeper than software research that is currently being conducted, because the problems addressed are inherently broader and deeper. The proposed research does not supplant current, important software research but rather significantly expands its horizons. We believe this research could result in operational capabilities to develop and evolve the ULS systems of the future. The envisioned outcome of the proposed research is a spectrum of technologies and methods for developing these systems of the future, with national-security, economic, and societal benefits that extend far beyond ULS systems themselves.

5 Summary and Recommendations

Our conclusion is that with appropriate investments, capable, reliable, and responsive ULS systems could be developed, validated, deployed, operated, and evolved. The United States needs to establish a program that will fund the software research needed to support the ongoing transformations in national defense and global interdependence. The key challenge is the decision to move forward. The ULS System Research Agenda presented in this report provides the starting point for the path ahead.

6
Detailed Description of Research Areas

In this section of the report, we describe more fully the research areas and topics that were introduced in Section 4. For each research area, we summarize why ULS systems require research in the area, briefly discuss related research topics, and recommend references for further reading about the topics.[21]

This collection of research areas and topics is not meant to be exhaustive. Rather it is representative of—and highlights promising directions for—the spectrum of research needed to address the current, imminent, and long-term challenges posed by ULS systems. Our goal in this section is to convey a sense of the breadth of research needed to develop ULS systems and to define opportunities for building a research program for ULS systems. We present a diverse range of research areas and topics, some relatively conservative with benefits likely in the short term and some of greater risk but promising more substantial benefits if successful.

6.1 Human Interaction

People and their organizations are essential components of ULS systems, which we have already characterized as socio-technical ecosystems. Many of the failures in complex systems today stem from failures at the individual and organizational level. ULS systems will present even greater challenges due to their inherently vast distribution and the expected absence of a single central administrative authority. Computer science and related engineering fields are not well equipped to address the interaction of technology with people, even in single, unconnected systems. When approaching the challenges associated with ULS systems, we must collaborate with and learn from anthropologists, sociologists, and social scientists.

21 The references we discuss in the "Further Reading" sections are not intended to be exhaustive or pose as a scholarly bibliography, but rather give a sample set of authoritative offerings that provide more information.

Behavioral analysis that is based on an economic model (for example, see Section 6.2.1 on algorithmic mechanism design) has the advantage of isolating one crucial factor: how the selfish pursuit of individual interest influences collective outcomes. But human behavior can also be studied to advantage using a cultural approach, focusing on the shared practices (and the beliefs that support them) used by members of work groups to organize their activities, whether mundane or exceptional. Indeed, a group's culture can be thought of as an evolving set of practices for accomplishing various activities. Practices are how things really get done in everyday life; in this sense, they must be distinguished from a group's rule-like laws and norms, which are intended to proscribe and regulate the everyday through formal, necessarily abstract statements about how things should ideally or authoritatively get done.

Moreover, groundbreaking interdisciplinary research by Hutchins (among others) demonstrates that many social processes are, in fact, computational processes, which yields an important insight in the opposite direction: computational processes, at least at the scale of a ULS system, are actually social processes. Hutchins' detailed description of navigation on a Navy vessel[22] demonstrates a view of computation that goes far beyond the digital computer. In this view, humans can be intrinsic elements of a socially constituted computational process. Computational processes are governed by protocols that are derived from and deeply embedded in specific cultures. In fact, these protocols are so deeply embedded as to be effectively invisible to the human actors. These culture-embedded protocols must be understood before they can be made explicit and must be made explicit before their digital elements can be made transparent to the human actors.

For example, every firm (and every family) performs a computational process of receiving and spending money every month. Society places constraints on these computations: firms (and families) that "fail" are deemed "bankrupt," and are subject to constraints and reorganization. "Balancing our books" is a very mundane but ubiquitous, socially constructed computational process.

We cannot fully anticipate the context within which ULS systems will operate and necessarily evolve, as the socio-cultural practices of many different groups (stakeholders, users) will, in fact, be constructing this real-world computational environment. The challenge is thus to design and support systems using an accurate model (scientific understanding) of this ULS/social-context interaction. What is needed, then, are detailed socio-technical analyses of user interactions, in the field, with complex sources of information that current large-scale systems make possible. Analyses of actual situations of decision making will help us to develop a more sophisticated understanding of the ways that computational environments with such systems are truly constructed.

Research into the human aspects of ULS systems is needed on the topics described below.

22 Hutchins, Edwin. *Cognition in the Wild.* Boston, MA: The MIT Press, 1995.

6.1.1 Context-Aware Assistive Computing

Research Tracks

Essential

(M1) (RT1)

(M2) (RT4)

(M3) (RT5)

(M3) (RT6)

A defining characteristic of a ULS system is an intentional blurring of the division between the physical and digital worlds. In particular, new input and output technologies create opportunities for computers to be more helpful to people doing complex tasks. ***Context-aware computing*** describes the situation in which a (possibly mobile) computer is aware of its users' state and surroundings and modifies its behavior based on this information.

A user's context can be quite rich, consisting of attributes such as physical location, physiological state (such as body temperature and heart rate), emotional state (such as angry, distraught, or calm), personal history, daily behavioral patterns, and so on. A human assistant given such context would make decisions proactively, anticipating users' needs. In making these decisions, the assistant would typically not disturb the user at inopportune moments except in an emergency. Similarly this assistant would filter, abstract, and visualize information to aid the user's decision making.

The goal of context-aware assistive computing is to enable (mobile) computers or intelligent environments to exploit context information to *assist* people by

- significantly reducing demands on their attention through adaptive automation, and
- providing them with the right information and easy-to-access control capabilities at the right time, for more effective manual task execution.

Combined with inferences about users' intentions, context-aware computing would enable improvement in user-perceived network and application performance and reliability. Context-aware applications are built on fundamental sensing services such as spatial and temporal awareness. Spatial awareness includes the relative and absolute position and orientation of a user. Temporal awareness includes the scheduled time of public and private events. Research in context-aware assistive computing should include the following subtopics:

Adapting to Changing User-Resource Needs. Many of the capabilities in ULS systems require adaptive behavior to meet user expectations and smooth the imbalances between demands and changing environments. There are two fundamental types of adaptation required: (1) changes beneath the applications to continue to meet the required service levels despite changes in resource availability and (2) changes at the application level to either react to currently available levels of service or request new levels under modified circumstances. In both, a ULS system must determine whether it needs to (or can) reallocate resources or change strategies to achieve the desired quality of service. We therefore need research to develop context-aware applications, ***middleware***, operating systems, and networks that can change their quality-of-service demands as the conditions under which they operate change. Mechanisms for reconfiguration must be put into place to implement new levels of quality of service as required, with attention to both the individual and the aggregate points of view and the conflicts that they may represent.

Adapting to Changing User Tasks. Just as user-resource needs will vary over time, so too will user tasks vary. In many cases, the ULS system will need to take the initiative to help the user work effectively. This transcends traditional system adaptation, which is typically a matter of resource allocation. Runtime reconfiguration may have the effect of altering parts of the system that are directly or indirectly visible to people and could therefore cause confusion. We therefore need research on mechanisms that moderate the effects of people-visible changes to the ULS system, or that adapt existing user views to the new system states. Research is also needed in context-aware technologies that can semantically model user tasks and goals and automatically provide or suggest alternative forms of data presentation, visualization, aggregation, and filtering. In addition, research is needed on modifying the task model itself, to take into account the users' needs and state.

6.1.2 Understanding Users and Their Contexts

Research Tracks

Essential	Support
M3 (RT5)	M1 (RT1)
M3 (RT6)	M1 (RT2)
	M2 (RT3)

The designers and developers of ULS system software cannot be expected to anticipate fully the context within which ULS systems will be built and operated and how they will evolve. This context will be continually changing, and there will be many different groups of stakeholders (such as users, application developers, acquirers, policy makers, tool and infrastructure makers, etc.), each of whom will have their own community and associated socio-cultural practices and expectations. Accurately understanding and capturing the user's context is already a difficult and error-prone task for existing systems, many of which fail because they are deemed unusable by their stakeholders. In the ULS context, the ever-changing nature of the system, its users, and its environment make this a far greater challenge. Meeting this challenge will require research to enable better integration of user modeling and ethnographic elicitation techniques, as discussed below.

Ethnographic Foundations for User-Centered Specifications. Individual users pursue their own objectives, and users are often unable to express or generalize these objectives outside the context of actual system use. Different users place their own values on specific services and have different expectations, which may be more or less stringent than the system's developers intended. Research on specification and evaluation methods and tools that help us consider the *context* and *expectations* of specific users and that build on existing techniques for questionnaires, interviews, and contextual inquiry can address this challenge. Research is needed to elicit and understand the users' needs and expectations, and to determine how to *structure* the elicitation of those expectations in a form that the user will find manageable.

Representing User Beliefs and Expectations. Because the set of user expectations will be far more complex in a ULS system than in a traditional system, we also need research in representing user knowledge and belief systems. This information must be represented in a way that is both comprehensible and capable of analysis, which is a further facet of the needed research. Last, we will need tools to model and predict whether a ULS system can meet its stakeholders' expectations, before the system is built or fielded.

Runtime Mechanisms for Assessing and Moderating User Beliefs and Expectations. In addition, context-dependent *runtime* mechanisms will be needed to determine whether the modeled expectations are being met by the running system and, if not, how to rectify the situation. Because these models will profoundly affect the operation of the system, research must validate that the models are usable and complete and that they faithfully represent the users' expectations.

6.1.3 Modeling Users and User Communities

Research Tracks

Essential	Support
M3 (RT6)	M1 (RT1)
	M1 (RT2)

To develop more sophisticated insights into how ULS systems are actually constructed and how they evolve, research is needed to construct user models and context models based on detailed socio-technical analyses of user interactions in the field:

Modeling Communities of Users Rather Than Individuals. While existing systems occasionally contain user models—for example, ***GOMS (goals, operators, methods, and selection rules) models***—they do not contain explicit models of groups or communities of users and their behaviors. Research would help us know how to make ULS systems serve such communities effectively.

Continuous User Modeling. The needs and preferences of users change as they use a software system. If the system is itself evolving as the users and their needs evolve, user modeling must be repeated. In particular it cannot succeed if it is solely a design-time activity. More research is therefore needed on the topic of ***universal usability:*** how to collect data about users with a wide variety of expertise and knowledge that is continuously and autonomously updated. And these models of users and their groups must be regularly updated without constant human intervention.

Representing the User and the Context. A ULS system will have to explicitly model the user's intention and context as well as organizational or enterprise goals and context. We therefore need research on the topic of contextual inquiry to improve our abilities to conduct and validate user studies, ethnographic studies, and system evaluations in real ULS systems.

Inferring Diverse User Needs and Utility. ULS systems should adapt their behaviors to the needs of users and their circumstances. Rules of engagement must be considered as part of the user's context, and policies governing system operation must be dynamically changeable. ULS systems serve diverse users with different needs at different times and with different fundamental relations to the system. These needs are independent and possibly at variance with those of other users. We therefore need research on topics such as universal access: accessibility guidelines, adaptive and augmented interaction, alternative input/output techniques, designing for diversity, modality-independent interaction, multi-sensory interfaces, and personalization.

6.1.4 Fostering Non-Competitive Social Collaboration

Research Tracks

Essential	Support
M1 (RT1)	M2 (RT4)
M1 (RT2)	M3 (RT5)
M3 (RT6)	

The motivations for individuals (and even firms) to engage in open-source projects are not exactly based on pure self-interests: included in the basis are human characteristics such as the need to share, to give and receive gifts, and to act altruistically.[23] Even in this arena, self-interests do have a place. They take the form of an interest in becoming well regarded, being thought of as productive and intelligent, and becoming known rather than in simply accumulating wealth. The open-source community participates in the larger software- and systems-production realm, and, in many cases, open-source code forms some of the best foundations for our computing infrastructure. This software is produced without explicit cost, in a distributed fashion, and with high quality.

23 See Raymond, E. *The Cathedral & the Bazaar: Musings on Linux and Open Source by an Accidental Revolutionary.* O'Reilly, 2001.

As a research topic, open-source software development brings up many interesting issues that have not been extensively explored in the past:

Social Foundations for Non-Competitive Social Collaboration. What are the social foundations for non-competitive collaboration? How is it possible to collaborate in a way that is almost entirely virtual, and how does this form of collaboration compare with face-to-face interaction? How does one build trust and negotiate conflicts in such a community? The extended nature of the open-source community also brings up questions of multi-cultural bridging.

Economic Foundations for Non-Competitive Social Collaboration. Given that the open-source community does not operate primarily from a financial motive, is there any place for value-based approaches to software development? How are priorities established? How are tradeoffs and schedule decisions made, particularly when they affect potentially vast (largely unpaid) resources? What is the comparable role for risk-seeking or risk-averse behavior that we see in financially motivated markets? What are the incentive structures for cooperative organizations?

6.1.5 Longevity

Research Tracks

Essential	Support
M1 (RT2)	M2 (RT4)
M2 (RT3)	
M3 (RT6)	

One of the consequences of scale in ULS systems is that they will exist for a very long time—decades at least. This longevity affects aspects of the system having to do with people. It means that organizations will need to be able to work on and with the ULS system for many years. Moreover, people and organizations will be coming and going constantly within the ULS ecosystem. Key research questions include the following:

Stability of Requirements. How will requirements reflect the changing nature of people within the ULS system over decades-long durations? While it is inevitable that requirements will change over time, requirements must be monitored and managed to ensure that no individual or organization can appreciably change the system without understanding, and perhaps getting approval from, the other participants. This implies the need for research into the archiving and retrieval of requirements (which will become enormous repositories over time), and more important, for research into automated support for analyzing these requirements so that the implications of new requirements can be assessed and requirements trends can be tracked.

Stable Organizational Structures. Given that organizations evolve and that organizations are composed of individuals, how can we define structures that will ensure that an organization's involvement with a ULS system is consistent in management, personnel, and strategic changes over time? Conversely, if it is determined that some organizational change is necessary (even though it creates a discontinuity with some aspects of the existing system), what are the principles for how the ULS system will adapt to these changes?

Maintenance of Design Information. How can a ULS system remain fresh as different generations of users, designers, and others join it?

Ease of Learning. Given its ecosystem nature, how will new people in a ULS system learn about the parts of the ULS system relevant to them?

6.1.6 Further Reading

Paul Dourish's book *Where the Action Is: The Foundations of Embodied Interaction* [Dourish 01a] is one of the most important recent writings on human-centered design. Dourish argues that design should not be about tasks and their requirements or about applications, or computing; but rather, it should be about (human) ***embodied interaction*** and thus be especially concerned with the problem of shared awareness, with the organization of social relationships, and with human emotions as socio-cultural products (rather than individual internal states). Dourish has also written useful papers on context-aware computing and, more generally, the entire concept of context (not what parameters define it, but rather what kind of entity it is and where it comes from) [Dourish 01b] and the problem of context and shared awareness in human-computer interaction [Dourish 98].

For field studies of human behavior, especially work activities and how they can inform computer system design (focusing here on the idea of work *practices* rather than processes), an essential volume is *Workplace Studies: Recovering Work Practice and Informing Systems Design* by Luff and colleagues [Luff 00a]. Christian Heath and Paul Luff's *Technology in Action* [Luff 00b] provides useful studies of the relationship between humans and technology.

Finally, Edwin Hutchins' *Cognition in the Wild* [Hutchins 95] is essential reading for anyone interested in a thoroughly social (rather than largely psychological) account of human cognition and reasoning, written from an anthropological perspective and drawing extensively on field studies of decision making and reasoning where technology plays an important role.

[Dourish 98] Dourish, P. & Button, G. "On 'Technomethodology': Foundational Relationships between Ethnomethodology and System Design." *Human-Computer Interaction 13* (1998): 395-432.

[Dourish 01a] Dourish, P. *Where the Action Is: The Foundations of Embodied Interaction*. Cambridge, MA: MIT Press, 2001.

[Dourish 01b] Dourish, P. "Seeking a Foundation for Context-Aware Computing." *Human-Computer Interaction 16* (2001): 229–241.

[Hutchins 95] Hutchins, E. *Cognition in the Wild*. Cambridge, MA: MIT Press, 1995.

[Luff 00a] Luff, P.; Hindmarsh, J. & Heath, C. (eds.). *Workplace Studies: Recovering Work Practice and Informing Systems Design*. Cambridge University Press, 2000.

[Luff 00b] Luff, P. & Heath, C. *Technology in Action*. Cambridge University Press, 2000.

6.2 Computational Emergence

ULS systems must satisfy the needs of participants at multiple levels of organization (i.e., from individual components and users to whole institutions). These participants will often behave opportunistically to meet their own mission requirements, irrespective of the goals and objectives of other participants. In such cases, methods and tools based on economics and ***game theory*** (e.g., ***mechanism design***) are likely to play an important role in ensuring the achievement of globally optimal behavior even when the participants are concerned only with achieving their own goals.

ULS systems must satisfy the needs of their users not only at any instant in time, but also across the lifespan of these systems as they evolve. ***Metaheuristics*** and ***digital evolution*** offer promising means to cope with pressures that require ULS systems to adapt to new environments, new policies, missions, and mechanisms. These techniques appear to have the potential to augment the cognitive limits of human designers and to find novel design solutions to complex design problems. Research can determine whether it will be possible for rules for continuous evolution to be built into ULS systems and their supporting ***platforms*** so that they can become more self-reliant and cope with dynamically changing environments without constant human intervention. These ideas suggest the need for research on ***in situ control, reflection, and adaptation*** to ensure continuous adherence to system policies despite rapidly changing operational demands and resource availability.

The technologies described here represent some of the more speculative research in this report. As a result, they may be constrained to relatively narrow domains of application in the early phases of ULS system research. They all, however, enlist the use of computational resources to solve important challenges in ULS system design and evolution, and they highlight a future state in which a synergy is achieved between digital and human participants in ULS systems.

6.2.1 Algorithmic Mechanism Design

Research Tracks

Essential

- M1 (RT1)
- M2 (RT3)
- M2 (RT4)
- M3 (RT5)
- M3 (RT6)

ULS systems will, in many cases, lack a central locus of operational or institutional control, and the participants in the system at any time (including users *and* institutions) will have disjointed and competing interests. A key challenge in this context is to provide a basis for simultaneously satisfying system-wide quality goals *and* satisfying the (competing) goals and expectations of many diverse actors. It is precisely these scale factors that point to a promising avenue of ULS systems research, namely research in applying economic theories of decentralized decision making to software systems. This research, one variant of which is known as mechanism design and another as ***institution design,*** lies at the intersection of ***microeconomics*** and game theory. It involves designing mechanisms, protocols, and institutions that are mathematically proven to satisfy certain system-wide objectives under the assumption that individuals interacting through such institutions act in a self-interested manner and may hold private information that is relevant to a required decision. Economic behavior yields the utility of cooperation from the discord of competition; mechanism design regards cooperation as an *emergent* property of agents engaging in selfish, competitive economic behavior. *Algorithmic* mechanism design puts mechanism design into a

> Mechanism Design:

Combining Game Theory, Microeconomics, and Computation

(A) GAME THEORY (1)

Oskar Morgenstern
1902 – 1977

Monograph Efficiency	9.3
Marginal Rate of Reference	0.0
Public Perception Indicator	1.8
Productivity Potential Index	-24.0
Expected Utility	1.5

(A) GAME THEORY (2)

John von Neumann
1903 – 1957

Monograph Efficiency	3.7
Marginal Rate of Reference	12.0
Public Perception Indicator	22.3
Productivity Potential Index	-44.0
Expected Utility	1.0

(A) GAME THEORY (3)

John F. Nash Jr.
b1928

Monograph Efficiency	0.0
Marginal Rate of Reference	0.0
Public Perception Indicator	11.1
Productivity Potential Index	+10.2
Expected Utility	5.0

(A) GAME THEORY (4)

Reinhard Selten
b1930

Monograph Efficiency	6.3
Marginal Rate of Reference	14.0
Public Perception Indicator	2.2
Productivity Potential Index	+11.4
Expected Utility	2.0

Relevance to DoD Missions

ULS systems must support warfighters at all echelons who are engaged in information-intensive activities and who must share critical but finite information technology resources. Future combat missions will require robust and decentralized resource allocation mechanisms that are resilient to deception, support a diversity of interests, and provide fully predictable and near-optimal global outcome.

Key Concepts

Game theory provides mathematical tools to study the outcomes of interactions among self-interested, and possibly deceptive, players, where the interactions are governed by a set of rules. *Mechanism design* is the inverse of game theory: it seeks to discover the rules of games that will result in a desired outcome despite self-interested and deceptive behavior. Mechanism design is concerned primarily with *microeconomics*—the economic behavior of agents in the face of scarcity.

computational setting: using computers to design mechanisms and using mechanisms to control computing.[24]

In a ULS system, mechanism design can be applied to problems involving the sharing of scarce or exclusive resources (e.g., network bandwidth, power) among actors—both human and computational—that may engage in strategic behavior marked by a combination of guile and self-interest. Mechanism design has a mathematical foundation and has seen many practical applications in settings ranging from many extremely small-scale transactions (e.g., eBay auctions) to a small number of extreme-scale transactions (e.g., allocating the U. S. radio spectrum). For these reasons, mechanism design holds promise for effecting emergent behavior in ULS systems. While mechanism design is a well-established field in its own right, we need the following fundamental research to apply the theory to ULS systems:

Computational Complexity of Algorithmic Mechanism Design. While mechanism design has a rich history, its embedding in computational settings is more recent. The cornerstone ***revelation principle*** (that is, the principle that a social-choice function can always be designed such that actors will truthfully reveal their preferences) may be valid in a strictly mathematical sense, but the computational complexity (these are typically ***NP-complete*** problems) for agents to compute their preferences may lead to inaccurate valuations, in turn leading to suboptimal global results. On the other hand (and for the same reason), computational complexity can be used to defeat strategic behavior (i.e., it affects honest and dishonest actors equally). Thus scale can have both positive and negative effects on mechanisms, and we need to understand these effects better. For application to ULS systems, many of the well-established possibility *and* impossibility results from the theory of mechanism design must be re-examined in light of computational complexity. In addition, research is needed to determine effective approximate algorithms, since, as systems grow to ultra-large scale, we will inevitably encounter situations where an NP-complete algorithm is impractical.

Computational Complexity of Automated Mechanism Design. Automated mechanism design—allowing the system to determine and optimize its own mechanisms—is essential in self-adapting systems but hampered by the complexity of design search. More research would help us understand the theoretical and practical limits of automated mechanism design. While the constrained subject area works to the advantage of design automation, computational complexity and the high confidence usually required of game-theoretic solutions are countervailing forces. In particular, it is important to know which subjects are suitable for automated mechanism design and for these subjects to obtain a sound means to estimate the rate of convergence of an automated design process to a desired (not necessarily optimal) quality goal. In this way, a reasoned tradeoff between the optimality and practicality of the designed mechanisms can be determined.

24 These ideas are closely related to the concepts of decentralized and competitive design processes described in Section 6.1, but concepts of mechanism design, in particular, make much stronger assumptions about the nature of the competing agents and about the game being played than are likely to hold in a world of competing design teams.

Adaptation as a Mechanism. Algorithmic mechanisms cannot be introduced simultaneously at all points in a ULS system. As a consequence, new mechanisms will have to co-exist with more traditional "pre-mechanistic" resource-management strategies. An important research question is how a ULS system can incorporate mechanisms *through which agents will adopt new mechanisms*. One issue that this research must address is how to motivate the adoption of new mechanisms in spite of possibly nontrivial switchover costs. A second issue is how to sustain switchover processes over time, for example through transition periods where scale limitations of older mechanisms diminish due to the adoption of new mechanisms.

Mechanisms for Acquisition. Online auction systems such as eBay are widely known, but they make use of just one class of mechanism—the auction. Other classes of mechanism are also being explored, some of which may have direct application not just to the control of ULS systems but also to their production and acquisition. For example, voting mechanisms enable an arbitrary society of agents to agree on actions that bind the entire society in virtual enterprises. Bargaining mechanisms allow bilateral agreements among agents that have conflicting interests, for example in subcontracting; contracts and ***contract nets*** are an important application. Market mechanisms enable efficient distribution of goods between two classes of agents: producers of software products and consumers of these products. Research is therefore needed in both the creation of novel mechanisms and the efficacy of mechanisms such as those discussed here.

6.2.2 Metaheuristics in Software Engineering

Research Tracks

Essential

M2 (RT4)

M3 (RT5)

Although algorithmic mechanism design is promising, it works best in situations in which the goals of individual participants can be precisely characterized. It is less well suited to situations in which participants themselves are attempting to satisfy multiple, possibly competing objectives that may change from time to time. Of course, this is also an ever-present problem in systems that is sometimes characterized as quality-attribute tradeoff. For example, while mechanism design might be suitable for providing guarantees of optimal allocation of network bandwidth under competing interests, it is not (yet) suitable for guaranteeing an optimal bandwidth allocation under competing quality requirements for security (e.g., data privacy) or reliability (e.g., data redundancy). Moreover, because mechanisms embody a priori solutions to design problems, they do not address another significant challenge posed by ULS systems—their longevity.

In effect, while mechanism designs provide optimal solutions for the ULS system at a particular instant in its evolution, they do not address a search for optimality in the (relatively) deep time of the overall life of a ULS system. To meet these challenges, research is needed on metaheuristics, which is a class of (often biologically inspired) search techniques that iteratively

> Metaheuristics:

Search with Ants, Swarms, and Genetics

Relevance to DoD Missions
War fighting poses many optimization problems (e.g., in logistics and movement control). Future combat situations will be ever more dynamic, and optimization decisions will be based on more data and more diverse types and sources of data. The ability to quickly generate near-optimal solutions to complex optimization problems will provide the future warfighter with a qualitative edge on the battlefield.

Key Concepts
Many critical optimization problems, for example finding the most time-efficient route for delivering material to a (possibly large) number of locations, are known to be computationally intractable. Rules of thumb—or *heuristics*—are search strategies used to find reasonable solutions with reasonable effort, though these solutions may be far from optimal. *Metaheuristics* are super-strategies that can combine, control, and guide the operation of lower level heuristics. Many metaheuristic strategies are inspired by optimization strategies found in biological systems (ant colonies) and physical processes (*annealing*).

seeks an optimum solution within a landscape of possibilities that may be extremely complicated and even discontinuous. Metaheuristics characterize a problem as a set of states within a search space, a current state, a ***mutator function*** (that moves from one state to another), and some objective (goal or fitness) function that is to be optimized. Common examples of metaheuristic techniques are ***genetic programming***, ***simulated annealing***, ***greedy algorithms***, ***swarm intelligence***, and ***ant-colony optimization***. Metaheuristics have already found several applications in software engineering research and development. The emphasis of metaheuristics is on simple parts that collectively solve a complex problem. For example, ants, slide molds, or individual neurons possess little intelligence and little context individually, but they react and adapt intelligently en masse over time. These examples suggest that metaheuristic techniques may be able to scale to ultra-large problems in a way that traditional software engineering techniques cannot.

Examples of existing uses of metaheuristics are found in software testing, algorithm optimization, and program analysis. We need research on the following topics associated with metaheuristics:

Representation of Software Engineering Problems as Metaheuristic Problems. Many problems in software engineering are not readily or obviously transformed into search problems. Test-data generation is an example of a software engineering problem that *has* been successfully treated using metaheuristics: this problem has a large, natural search component and an easily definable ***fitness function***. For example, in ***clear-box testing***, a natural and easily defined fitness function is the percentage of branches that have been covered by the test suite. Research will determine the broad class of software engineering problems that can be naturally understood and represented as search problems.

Creating Objective Functions. Can ***objective functions***—the measures that metaheuristic algorithms use to direct their searches—be easily and naturally specified? One approach is to harness the techniques used in ***test-driven design*** disciplines in which part or all of a specification is in terms of user-understandable tests residing in a simple test harness. Can a more adaptable approach to objective functions be found? Can we learn from the recent research in biology on ***hypermutation***—the mechanism by which the human immune system adapts to new attacks—and the regulation of mutations under stress?

Creating Mutator Functions. Mutator functions are the engine that moves the search from one state in the space to another. Creating such functions is currently a handcrafting process. For the metaheuristic approach to be widely applicable, research is needed that guides the developer in mapping from the problem space to an *effective* mutator function.

Harnessing Swarm Intelligence. Ant-colony optimization (and related algorithms) and ***particle swarm optimization*** are two successful techniques using swarm intelligence: the study of collective behavior in decentralized, self-organized systems such as swarms, flocks, schools, and herds. Research is needed to apply swarm intelligence to ULS resource management, quality-attribute maintenance, and robustness in general. Swarm intelligence is appropriate in situations where there are large numbers of relatively inexpensive, relatively autonomous agents that collectively need to solve some search or optimization problem.

6.2.3 Digital Evolution

Research Tracks

Essential	Support
M2 (RT3)	M3 (RT5)
M2 (RT4)	
M3 (RT6)	

Human cognition constrains designers to consider designs that are elegant, understandable, modular, and mostly hierarchical. Good designs for some parts of ULS systems, however, might well be found in less-well-structured design spaces. In such cases, machines might be able to produce better designs than people. The objective of ***digital software evolution*** is to use the brute power of computers to overcome the constraining limits of human cognition to discover optimal or unusual, ***satisficing*** engineering solutions, at the cost of design-time qualities such as the understandability of a design.

Digital software evolution uses metaheuristic techniques such as genetic programming and simulated annealing to design and implement software that exhibits desired emergent behavior. At present, most work on digital software evolution is centered on the creation of algorithms or entire programs. The results, both theoretical and practical, have been good so far, but the following types of research are needed to enable digital software evolution to work effectively on the larger, more complex components in ULS systems:

Evolving Designs Through Crossover. Can ***crossover***, which is the process of combining traits from two individuals in the population that is being evolved, be optimized to better capture good partial designs, perhaps in a manner akin to automatically defined functions and ***speciation*** but using human designs as well as digitally evolved designs? This approach aims at automating only part of the design process rather than all of it. Proven designs would be the raw material used by digital software evolution to essentially compose or combine known designs into larger and more complex ones. Moreover, perhaps designs produced by digital software evolution can be used as material for higher level (human and nonhuman) designs. We also note that metaheuristic concepts might have applications to manual design processes. For example, the concept of crossover might well have applications to iterated competitions between design organizations (as discussed in Section 6.1), where at certain points some teams can see what other teams have done and adopt successful elements as a starting point for a next round.

Evolvable Resource-Sharing Policies. In deployed ULS systems, unexpected interactions between components through resource sharing—including such things as power usage on portable, power-poor devices—can lead to difficult-to-diagnose problems. It might be possible to treat resource sharing as a first-class evolvable entity and apply crossover, mutation, etc. to this aspect of the system, either as a resource or as part of a process that boosts robustness and stability.

Evolvable Modularization. People design systems by fixing interfaces early and by modularizing based on limiting the number of function points in a module. Can better, more robust designs evolve when the definitions of modules can vary by allowing functionality to be moved from module to module or to be replicated entirely? Digital software evolution may be able to exploit such situations—in fact, a problem encountered in genetic programming, especially in designing analog circuits, is that accidental functionalities are unexpectedly exploited.

Automatically Evolved Intercomponent Glue. A simple problem in producing a working system from a high-level design is producing the ***glue*** that connects components together. The details of an application programming interface (API) can cause numerous problems, particularly when the API evolves. How much of a system's intercomponent glue can be evolved automatically? This problem includes being able to discover proper API conventions and protocols as well as scaffolding code.

Automatically Evolved Implementations. A problem with software development as it is practiced today is that, while the overall design of a program or component might be fine, the details can be tricky. Is it possible to use software evolution to complete the implementation of a design once a certain level of detail is achieved? Can features, performance, or other characteristics be continuously and automatically improved or ***refactored*** through a process of slow, conservative software evolution? Can evolutionary techniques based on possible refactorings be used to find good, effective parallelizations of single-threaded code?

Regulating Digital Evolution. Is it possible to combine approaches to gain better overall performance of software evolution by using various regulation mechanisms? For example, some researchers have tried combining genetic programming with ***Bayesian techniques*** to try to quell the tendency for genetic programming to create larger and larger programs as the number of generations grows. Genetic mechanisms may provide clues for other concepts. For example, in nature, the production of a *phenotype* (an organism) given a *genotype* (genetic code) involves a lengthy process controlled by several regulatory mechanisms. Can we find and harness similar regulatory mechanisms to improve digital software evolution by creating regulated distance between the representation that evolution manipulates and the resulting program? Current research into ***type-safe staged computation*** is a preliminary step in this direction. Recently it has been observed that mutation rates and the loci of mutations in a genome can be modulated under stress (adverse changing environmental conditions). Perhaps our metaheuristic algorithms including digital software evolution can benefit from similar mechanisms.

Self-Sustaining Techniques. The work of keeping a system healthy and alive is not always the same as the designed operation of that system. Some promising approaches are detecting non-self in the behavioral domain using immunological techniques, detecting damaged or inconsistent data structures and performing (minimal) repairs, and performing micro-reboots of suspected components. To sustain a long-running system, can we use continual re-creation techniques, such as ***autopoiesis*** and ***autocatalysis***? An autopoietic system is one whose network of components and the components are continually produced by that network of components; an autocatalytic system is a chemical reaction whose required catalyst is produced by the reaction itself.

6.2.4 Further Reading

Nisan and Ronen's "Algorithmic Mechanism Design" [Nisan 99] is the seminal paper on computational mechanisms. Although this paper appeared several years after various prototypical applications of mechanisms in computing settings, it provided a definite structure for further research. Sandholm's "Distributed Rational Decision Making" [Sandholm 99] is an accessible survey of computational mechanisms, covering voting, auctions, bargaining, markets, and contract nets. Schneidman and Parkes [Schneidman 03] explain the use of mechanisms to overcome naturally occurring strategic behavior in peer-to-peer networks and outline a number of open problems that remain to be solved. Blum and Roli provide a concise overview, classification, and comparison of research in metaheuristics [Blum 03]. A book-level treatment of just one population-based metaheuristic is available in Dorigo and Stutzle's *Ant Colony Optimization* [Dorigo 04].

The de rigueur references on genetic programming and ***genetic algorithm*** are the books by John Koza and his colleagues [Koza 92, Koza 94, Koza 99, Koza 03]. Papers indicative of the practical application of digital evolution and the range of nonhuman design are by Adrian Thompson and his colleagues [Thompson 99, Thompson 02].

[Blum 03] Blum, C. & Roli, A. "Metaheuristics in Combinatorial Optimization: Overview and Conceptual Comparison." *ACM Computing Surveys 35*, 3 (September 2003): 268-308.

[Dorigo 04] Dorigo, M. & Stutzle, T. *Ant Colony Optimization*. Cambridge, MA: MIT Press, 2004.

[Koza 92] Koza, J. *Genetic Programming: On the Programming of Computers by Means of Natural Selection*. Cambridge, MA: MIT Press, 1992.

[Koza 94] Koza, J. *Genetic Programming II: Automatic Discovery of Reusable Programs*. Cambridge, MA: MIT Press, 1994.

[Koza 99] Koza, J.; Bennett, F.; Andre, D.; & Keane, M. *Genetic Programming III: Darwinian Invention and Problem Solving*. San Francisco, CA: Morgan Kaufmann, 1999.

[Koza 03] Koza, J.; Keane, M.; Streeter, M.; Mydlowec, W.; Yu, J.; & Lanza, G. *Genetic Programming IV: Routine Human-Competitive Machine Intelligence*. Norwell, MA: Kluwer Academic Publishers, 2003.

[Nisan 99] Nisan, N. & Ronen, A. "Algorithmic Mechanism Design," 129-140. *Proceedings of the 31st ACM Symposium on Theory of Computing*. Atlanta, GA, May 1–4, 1999.

[Sandholm 99] Sandholm, T. "Distributed Rational Decision Making," 201–258. *Multiagent Systems: A Modern Introduction to Distributed Artificial Intelligence*. Weiss, G., ed. Cambridge, MA: MIT Press, 1999.

[Schneidman 03] Shneidman, J. & Parkes, D. "Rationality and Self-Interest in Peer to Peer Networks." *Proceedings of the 2nd International Workshop on Peer-to-Peer Systems (IPTPS '03)*. Berkeley, CA, Feb. 20–21, 2003. Berlin, Germany: Springer-Verlag, 2003.

[Thompson 99] Thompson, A.; Layzell, P.; & Zebulum, R. "Explorations in Design Space: Unconventional Electronics Design Through Artificial Evolution." *IEEE Transactions of Evolutionary Computation 3*, 3 (September 1999): 167–196.

[Thompson 02] Thompson, A. "Notes on Design Through Artificial Evolution: Opportunities and Algorithms," 17–26. *Adaptive Computing in Design and Manufacture V*. Berlin, Germany: Springer-Verlag, 2002.

6.3 Design

Designing software for ULS systems involves activities such as the following:

- participating in the formulation of the problems that the systems will address as they relate to the software elements;
- defining the capabilities required in the software to address such needs;
- structuring and developing plans (or *designs* in the narrow sense of the word[25]) for producing such software; and
- regulating the production of the software, evaluating it, and making changes as information and conditions change.

Current design theory, methods, notations, tools and practices, and the acquisition methods that support them are inadequate to design ULS systems effectively. Some of the most important shortcomings are the following:

- Typical traditional design approaches are relatively centralized,[26] but centralized processes perform poorly at the complexity scale of ULS systems. This characterization is likely to be true for many aspects of ULS system software development, from determining requirements to detailed programming to support, maintenance, and evolution.

25 For ULS systems, designing encompasses producing the code for the system, not only making a plan for that code.

26 Although open source is not centralized and agile methodologies are not as centralized as many other methodologies, these approaches are usually considered outside the mainstream; however, there is a lot to learn from them for ULS systems.

- Much traditional software research and practice seeks methods enabling individual projects to produce good designs reliably on time and under budget—and, in some cases, projects succeed when measured this way. ULS system design, however, will be characterized by inherent uncertainty and incomplete knowledge of requirements and the consequences of design decisions. ***Design risk*** is inherent. Therefore nearly every project—even competently executed projects—will exhibit significant variation (i.e., unpredictability) in costs, duration, and quality of results.
- Although traditional design methods are formulated to facilitate design evolution, the impact of change in many dimensions and across many time scales without the control of centralized design processes will pose particular problems for ULS systems. Moreover, although current design methods do emphasize design for change, they provide little guidance on how to invest in flexibility and generality in design.
- Today we have a poor understanding of the influence of economic conditions on design activities and thus in particular on how to establish economic conditions (e.g., through the organization of acquisition processes, incentives, and industry structures) conducive to producing good designs. We especially lack a clear understanding of how to fund design in the context of emergent requirements and the need for decentralized design processes. Similarly, we don't understand how to enlist the open-source, university and other software- and system-producing communities by means of their fundamental motivations to produce good designs.
- ULS system designs must satisfy combinations of demanding technical constraints that are difficult to satisfy even in today's relatively simple systems and for which, in some cases, requisite supporting infrastructure and mechanisms do not yet exist. Examples include simultaneous dependability, significant self-reconfigurability, and economic value. Reconfigurability greatly expands behavioral complexity, making static analysis and testing for high-assurance dependability costly at best, and infeasible in some cases.
- ULS systems will be both software intensive *and* human intensive, so the software elements must be designed with attention to issues ranging from technology to information processing by individual people, human teams, and organizations. Current software-design theories assume that the target environment is a network of computers and devices. Yet teams and human organizations within larger systems are also information-processing mechanisms, engendering new opportunities and complexities. We have little in the way of a theory for or practice of "engineering" human organizations.

Successful ULS systems will require substantial advances in theories, models, concepts, tools, technologies, methods, and applications of software design to address the challenges described above. The following research topics emerge from the need for these advances.

6.3.1 Design of All Levels

Research Tracks

Essential

(M2) (RT3)

(M3) (RT5)

(M3) (RT6)

The successful design of ULS systems appears to depend to a significant extent on the ***design of all levels***: not only of the software artifacts but of entire socio-technical ecosystems—both those that produce the systems and those in which they are employed—and of the linkages that integrate them into an even larger system. Design at all levels means designing the software artifacts, the development and acquisition infrastructure, and the rules and policies as a unit. Moreover, the complexity of ULS system design dictates the need for significant decentralization of design-production activities. For example, multiple industry sectors, each driven by competition and coordinated with each other by architectural agreements and other rules, constraints, and incentives, might be more effective in producing ULS system designs and improving them than traditional prime/subcontractor structures. The personal computer (PC) industry provides an example of such a decentralized design process. Multiple competitors within subsectors develop competing designs at the component level: for CPUs, operating systems, networks, and applications. The complexity of the PC is such that no single company could have advanced its design to the point at which it exists today. Monolithic PC designs could have been produced and were produced. However, it seems unlikely that any single company could have achieved the rapid, simultaneous advances we have seen in quality, cost, and performance in so many dimensions. The competition between Intel and AMD has produced tremendous advances in processor technology. A company the size of Microsoft has succeeded with just a few key system components: an operating system and an application suite. Another industry sector focuses on graphics hardware, another on sound cards, and so forth. The key idea is that a massive, decentralized industry structure, coordinated by architectural and other agreements and by other means but without a commanding centralized controller, now drives an extraordinary design process that continues to improve the PC. The PC, of course, is but one component type in a ULS system. We foresee the need for research on whether comparable industry structures and design processes could be harnessed to design ULS systems and components and on how to design them.

In addition to the design of ULS system artifacts and architectures, we would have to give attention to the design of the decentralized industrial and other organizations[27] that would develop and continually enhance these designs as well as to the design of the surrounding economic and other motivational

27 Such organizations include open-source communities, university and industrial research laboratories, and even individuals who produce high-quality designs and software based on motivations that are not purely monetary or even economic.

conditions; these include but are not limited to acquisition structures and methods. We therefore need research on theories and methods of design that relate detailed designs, architectural designs, decentralized organizations, and driving economic and other motivational forces. For example, we need new methods for developing and assessing the designs of end-to-end system architectures that will produce and continually improve ULS system designs.

6.3.2 Design Spaces and Design Rules

Research Tracks

Essential	Support
M2 (RT3)	M1 (RT2)
M2 (RT4)	M3 (RT5)
M3 (RT6)	

The architecture of a ULS system will consist of ***design rules*** (such as agreements on conventions, presuppositions, and constraints in the form of interfaces, standards, service-level agreements, etc.) that serve to decompose a system into component parts by decoupling design decisions that would otherwise be coupled. Design rules thereby also define the structure of the ***design spaces*** that will be explored by organizations working to design individual parts. The design process emerges as a search for valuable designs for both individual parts and combinations of parts, augmented by additional processes that occasionally select best-of-breed designs for parts and combinations thereof for testing and actual production. The architecture both divides the design work into simpler tasks and structures the design spaces that the competing organizations explore.

> Design Rules:

Combining Software and Engineering Systems Design, Financial Economics, and Complex Adaptive Systems

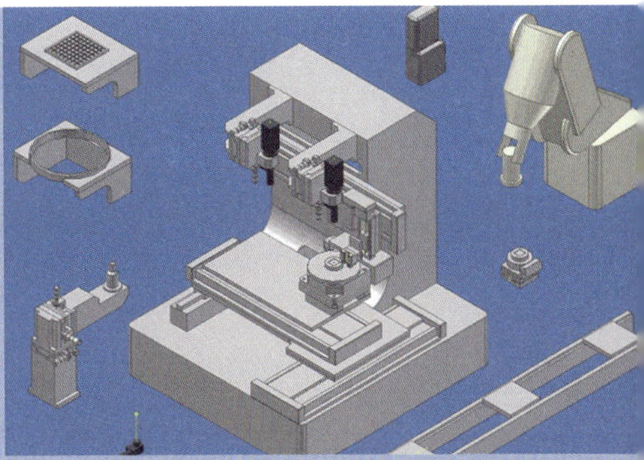

Relevance to DoD Missions

Mission-critical ULS systems will necessarily be developed and maintained over long periods of time by collections of organizations from various industry sectors. Today we lack a testable and validated theory of how to create incentives for development of an optimal or even viable allocation of design parts and processes to various industry and DoD constituents so that feasible ULS systems are produced.

Key Concepts

Modularity in design is a key to managing the complexity of software and to producing software systems amenable to change and to concurrent development. We are now learning that modularity also creates economic forces that shape and constrain large-scale design activities. Modules appear to create *real options,* capital investment analogs of financial options. Baldwin and Clark's concept of *design rules* provides a generalized account of what it means for a design to be modular and of the conditions under which such modularity generates significant economic potential. Design rules impose structure on design space to be searched for good solutions, allowing separate industry participants to seek good solutions independently within modules. As improved solutions are found, design transformations are made. The overall result is to organize the search for good system designs as a decentralized, *complex adaptive system.* Key research needs in this area are to develop, test, and apply descriptive theories to advance actual ULS system and software engineering capabilities.

This is a new perspective: architecture is not purely a technical plan for producing a single system or closely related family of systems, but a structuring of the design spaces that a complex design process at an industrial scale will explore over time. Note that although breaking up an architecture into design spaces and striving for a set of coherent and effective design rules would seem to imply a significant degree of control of the overall design and production process, the design spaces, design rules, and the organizations will be continually adjusting and adapting to both internal and external forces.

We need research on the methods and processes for devising ULS architectures in terms of design spaces and design rules. In particular, we need research on designing, representing, and analyzing design spaces. The design process is to explore the design space using parallel, decentralized processes regulated by design rules, which are architectural agreements and other constraints (such as security and performance) and incentives. Design rules must operate at many levels of abstraction—ranging from the outermost, most general shape of the architecture down to some level of detail below which possibly independent designers or design groups are permitted to make their own decisions.

Key research questions include the following:

Design Spaces. How do we support a design-space view of architecture with new representations, tools, and environments? How do we map, represent, and analyze the architectures of ULS systems to predict economic and technical properties of the resulting processes and products? How and to what extent do demanding performance requirements and other constraints limit the possibilities for modularization of architectures for ULS system designs? How can organizations leverage architecture for competitive advantage?

Design Rules. What are the means by which design rules for ULS systems are created and changed? How are design rules ***validated*** with respect to system-level properties that they are meant to assure, and how are the products produced by individual organizations during the process ***verified*** against prevailing design rules? How are design dependencies managed across component and organizational boundaries? How do we make design rules flexible enough to permit effective exploration of the design space over competing architectures (competing design rules)? How do we design ***attribute-specific design rules***, such as rules that lead to components that are not only secure in themselves but that remain secure when composed?

6.3.3 Harnessing Economics to Promote Good Design

Research Tracks

Essential	Support
M2 (RT3)	M1 (RT1)
	M1 (RT2)
	M2 (RT4)
	M3 (RT6)

Today we have few tested theories or practices of how to design ULS systems for economic value or of how to establish economic forces that promote good design, such as through new contracting structures. For example, we have no tested theory describing how modular architectures create economic value, and thus we have little scientific basis for designing modular industry structures that are likely to produce good designs for ULS systems and their parts. We therefore need research leading to a deeper understanding of how to organize designs and design activities to maximize value and of how to create economic conditions that predictably provide incentives to create valuable designs (net of the cost and time to produce them).

The decomposition of a ULS system into parts is likely to be of little use if there is no company that can profit by producing key parts; nor are high-quality parts likely to be produced with great economic efficiency in the absence of competition.[28] We lack a theory and practice of ***competitive software design***—i.e., of design processes in which competition is intentionally introduced at many levels. Likewise, we have little tested theory or practice of ***design risk*** management. If the outcome of a design attempt is uncertain, diversification over multiple independent attempts is an obvious strategy for risk management (as well as being consistent with the introduction of competition systematically into design processes). Indeed bakeoffs and other competitions are used today. We need research on how much diversity maximizes expected returns, how to promote design diversity in competitions, and how to use competition in detailed design.

Example research questions include the following:

Design Risk Management. When is diversification through parallel, competitive design-space exploration a better strategy for achieving goals in scope, cost, timeliness, and quality than previous attempts to develop repeatable design methods that reliably produce good outcomes? To what extent can we assume that multiple versions are independent in dimensions that matter (a question related to earlier work on assumptions of independence in the use of ***n-version programming*** to improve software reliability)? How can we quickly tell when designs are unlikely to succeed, and how can we organize our design processes to enable effective value-creating cancellation of unsuccessful designs?

Value Assessment. How do we model and use the value propositions of system users, producers, and others in formulating designs and design processes for economic viability? How can we assess the economic viability of proposed modules or system architectures? By what means can we design ULS systems when market forces are simply inadequate to provide an incentive for efficient design processes?[29]

28 Note that this discussion is solely in the context of commercial interests. Open-source projects, for example, produce high-quality software through a different process. In this report, we assume that open source will be part of the overall marketplace of software components and that the effects of competition between commercial and open-source projects will be similar to those described here in purely economic terms.

29 This can happen when a potential market for a system, part of a system, or component is too small or nonexistent. On the other hand, there is no requirement that design processes be efficient.

6.3.4 Design Representation and Analysis

Research Tracks

Essential	Support
M3 (RT6)	M1 (RT2)
	M2 (RT4)
	M3 (RT5)

Today's design representations do not support the kinds of design-theory development or practical analysis needed to support ULS system design. Key research questions include the following:

Design Rule Representation. How do we represent architectural designs based on generalized concepts of design rules and design spaces, rather than on the much more limited special case of APIs, which dominate in architectural design today?

Design Rule Properties. How do we analyze such new representations to ascertain likely technical and economic properties of designs and design processes?

Role Representation. How do we represent the information-processing, storage, and communications roles that people play in complex systems, perhaps in a manner that unifies modeling of human and information-technology elements?

Temporal Representation. How do we represent and validate temporal properties of design processes such as synchronization rules pertaining to separate companies and organizations?

Representing Diverse Parts. How can we construct detailed representations of designs whose parts are developed by separate—often competing—organizations?

Evaluating Representations for People. How can we evaluate tradeoffs among representation expressiveness, human comprehensibility, and the propensity for human error?

Today's design representations, which are based mostly on computational processes communicating through APIs, are far from sufficient to support the needs of ULS systems. For example, they do not readily admit representation of the design rules that have to be followed to enable secure interoperability.

6.3.5 Assimilation

Research Tracks

Essential	Support
M2 (RT3)	M1 (RT1)
M2 (RT4)	M3 (RT5)
M3 (RT6)	

Today's large-scale systems are often characterized by attempts to leverage components that were not designed to work together or that are inconsistent with the design rules of the architecture in which they are being inserted. It is doubtful, however, that force fitting uncoordinated components will scale up reliably to meet the demanding technical and economic requirements of ULS systems. Experience with today's systems-of-systems programs suggests that ULS systems will continue to face many similar problems, including the need to include legacy systems and the need to integrate and interact with off-the-shelf parts. Moreover, as ULS systems come to depend on third-party-provider network-based services, entirely new forms of old problems will emerge. Past research on techniques for dealing with such problems has not been commensurate with the magnitude of the problems, and the success of ULS systems likely depends on significant progress being made on ULS system assimilation, where nonconformant parts are assimilated into architecturally coherent ULS systems. To achieve this progress, the following research is needed:

6.3.5.1 Legacy-System Assimilation

Much of the work in developing and maintaining ULS systems will involve assimilating large legacy code bases—for example, by adding to those systems to create the basis for a ULS system, by reconfiguring the legacy system before insertion in a ULS system, and by redeploying legacy systems in contexts for which they were not designed as part of a ULS system. Significant changes will have to be made to existing legacy systems (for example, to change basic aspects of the system's functionality or design assumptions) in order to bring them into conformance with design rules sufficient to enable integration into a ULS system with reasonable assurance that required system properties will be attained or preserved. It is essential to find ways to exploit new technologies and social practices so that legacy systems describe their own structure and behavior more fully than they do today, with little additional burden on developers, so that they do not become ossified and incapable of evolution.

Each ULS system will exist for so long that some parts of it will become like legacy systems with respect to the emerging and evolving ULS system over time. The Y2K crisis is an apt, if perhaps overused, example of the problem. In the 1960s and 1970s (and even through the 1980s), many large-system developers believed that years (as dates) could be represented with two digits, reasoning that those systems would be replaced before any effects of the change of century resulted. No precautions were taken to make a simple conversion to a new or expanded representation when the time came. The result was that billions of dollars were spent to bring these systems up to date or to replace them when such replacements were not strictly necessary. This example raises numerous issues for ULS systems requiring research. It is not that the designers of the two-digit systems were irresponsible or poor designers; they chose the designs with deliberate thought and with knowledge of the limitations of the design decision, but made a tradeoff that was later to be regretted. Even today, excellent designers design with data-size limits when there are (computationally expensive) means to avoid these issues. We therefore need new research in the following topics:

Working with Legacy Code. We should develop techniques that enable analyzing, modeling, and evolving legacy code bases. The goals of such research include making it possible to model legacy code in various ways, to overlay models onto code, and to manipulate code by way of such models.

Working with Diverse Data. We must be able to exploit rich new capabilities in areas of ***metadata***, loosely structured data, multimedia, information search and synthesis, etc., to produce systems that have understandable, built-in design and operational diagrams and other documentation, produced without undue effort, and that are sufficient to help reduce the decay of structure and knowledge that cripples so many engineers of large systems today.

Working with Code Maturing into Legacy. We need to develop techniques to treat older parts of a ULS system as legacy, including how to handle unforeseen requirements, changing data characteristics, new technologies, etc.

6.3.5.2 Integrating Diverse and Uncertain Information Sources

ULS systems will often use information from diverse sources that varies in reliability and trustworthiness. The resulting aggregate information may therefore be inconsistent and it may be ***non-monotonic***: values may change and reliability may decrease as new information is integrated. Moreover, since the sources of information will be independent, the content, format, and other properties of the data will be subject to unpredictable change over time.

Some information sources must be integrated immediately, based on metadata and other formal descriptions. In some cases, rule sets will be integrated, and if they are proven unreliable, the conclusions reached and actions taken based on them must be addressed.

We need research on **Techniques for Integrating Diverse Information Sources.** We must be able to integrate information from multiple, diverse, and possibly unreliable or untrustworthy services, possibly immediately; determine the quality of the result; and adapt to variations in quality and to other changes over time.

Possible approaches to this requirement include the following:

- **Defining Standards for Information Sources.** We could define standards for describing information sources that include sufficient meta-information to set expectations about format, semantics, and availability.
- **Composing Information Sources.** We could create smart ***glue*** that monitors information sources to ensure that they behave as expected, taking remedial action if they do not.
- **Estimating Reliability of Information Sources.** We need to develop techniques for estimating the reliability of an integrated body of information that reflects the reliability of its individual sources.
- **Measuring Capabilities.** We need to generate measures of ULS system creation, evolution, operation, and support that reflect overall capability and permit identification of significant deviations at any system level.

6.3.5.3 Off-the-Shelf Components

As noted, for economic and technical reasons, ULS systems will be subject to pressures to incorporate ***off-the-shelf (OTS) components***[30] (which may be packaged as commercial, open source, government rights, etc.). A component is considered OTS if it was not designed, produced, and changed under the design rules that govern the system in which it is inserted. Components often include the teams/firms that developed them (through maintenance and service relationships, business acquisitions, etc). Models of assimilation in socio-technical ecosystems thus include not just technical means of assimilation such as software wrappers, but also business means, such as mergers and acquisitions, that provide new levels of design control.

Research questions include the following:

Effective Technical and Economic Decisions for OTS components. What tools, methods, theories, and technical and business practices can better enable designers to make technically and economically effective decisions regarding the use of OTS components in ULS systems and system components?

Assessing Quality Tradeoffs for OTS Components. What kinds of tools and practices are needed to assess quality tradeoffs and implications in all relevant dimensions, including reliability, availability, safety, security, risk of obsolescence, and life-cycle costs and benefits, especially concerning cost of change and of refreshing technology?

Assimilating OTS Components. How can OTS components be better assimilated into ULS systems when they are judged to be the best options?

30 The term "component" here is intended to mean a constituent part of the ULS system, which could be a web service or a piece of hardware.

Understanding Long-Term Value of OTS Components. How can situations in which the short-term benefits of using OTS components are outweighed by the present value of downstream costs under reasonable assumptions about the future be easily be recognized?

6.3.5.4 Component-Integration Technologies

Because not much can be done in the short term to change the direction of the installed base of hardware and software components, a reasonable approach is to provide the needed services at higher levels of ULS component-integration technologies, such as middleware platforms. A crucial issue is how to go beyond building component technologies for ULS systems that simply provide a better network, operating system, resource manager, or security service in isolation. We therefore need research on the following topics:

Integrating Components. We need techniques for *integrating* capabilities and delivering them to applications in ways that enable them to realize a model of adaptive behavior with tradeoffs among the various quality attributes. A promising approach is middleware that can be placed on top of legacy systems to take advantage of redundancy and diversity, acting as a coordinator for a variety of previously uncoordinated components—perhaps components that were never conceived of as being part of the same ULS system.

Hardware for ULS Component Integration. We need to look at new hardware and software platforms (computer systems, memory structures, specialized processors, frameworks, etc.) to support ULS system development and deployment.

6.3.5.5 Design for Assimilation

Today's software-design methods are largely based on the idea of composition of ***black-box abstractions***: components characterized by minimal external interfaces and implemented by hidden inner mechanisms. Some recent research (for example, on open implementations and ***aspect-oriented programming***) suggests that system assimilation might be eased by relaxing such strictly enforced abstraction. We need research on the following topics:

Dimensions of Design Assimilation. What tradeoffs are involved (for example, for and against ease of change) in the use of such approaches?

Mechanisms for Assimilation Design. What is the range of software-design techniques and mechanisms that can help to assimilate components into systems even if such components do not conform to all the design rules necessary for intervention-free integration or interoperation? Which approaches are best, and how can they be advanced?

6.3.6 Determining and Managing Requirements

Research Tracks

Essential

(M1) (RT2)

(M2) (RT3)

(M3) (RT5)

Formulating system requirements is a critical success factor in software engineering, and shortcomings in this dimension are one leading cause of software project failures. Determining or discovering the requirements is also the software engineering activity that is the most domain specific, the least capable of being automated and formalized, and the least scalable. ULS systems will make these problems worse because of the scope of application domains that exceed the limits of human intellectual capabilities, the complexity and fragmentation of socio-economic processes and organizations that are highly decentralized and autonomous, and the sheer complexity of the problems being addressed.

Because of the smaller scope and scale of traditional systems, it was sometimes workable for teams first to analyze requirements and write down specifications, and then to proceed through detailed design, coding, testing, etc.[31] For ULS systems, however, such a life cycle is unrealistic. Analysis and design methods must accommodate pervasive incompleteness, imperfection, uncertainty, and non-determinacy in the products and processes that arise throughout the system's development and evolution. The distinction is blurred between design time, development time, and runtime (or deployment time). We need research on ULS system requirements on such topics as the basics of requirements gathering, conflict management, ambiguity tolerance, and requirements phaseout.

6.3.6.1 Basics of Requirements Gathering

Because ULS systems comprehend so much functionality and therefore are unfathomably complex, requirements gathering takes on a whole new complexion. There will be, in effect, randomness or uncertainty in the requirements, in the specifications, and in the system itself—and it may not be possible to determine reliably where the problem lies. Further, because ULS systems will be socio-technical ecosystems, the scope of requirements gathering must expand to include people. Therefore we need research on the following:

User-Centered Requirements. We must understand ***user-centered design*** in the presence of diverse stakeholders including large numbers of diverse users with varying abilities and required tasks.

Implementing Partial Requirements. We must figure out how to do incremental or ***fractal*** design and implementation (perhaps in the mold of ***agile methodologies***).

Design Rules and Requirements Feedback. We must figure out how to construct design rules that encourage sophisticated feedback paths in requirements, specifications, designs, and implementations.

31 The category of a system can influence how feasible it is to gather requirements accurately before design and implementation. In some scientific and engineering situations, complete requirements are more likely to be determined beforehand than in situations where the deployment of the system alters social, organizational, or business forces in an ecosystem or society. In the latter case, requirements will tend to drift, and perhaps the entire ecosystem—the deployed system and its social and other components—will converge at some point.

6.3.6.2 Conflict Management

Because ULS systems will serve different classes of users with distinct interests, it will be difficult to detect and resolve conflicts in requirements for different system parts and stakeholders. We therefore need research on the following:

Competing Human Interests. We need to figure out how to represent, analyze, and reconcile distinct and competing interests. Examples include the following:

- developing logics that support multi-layered representation and reasoning;
- reconciling conflicting security requirements;
- reconciling requirements arising from users (user-centered design) and from those arising from non-user stakeholders; and
- analyzing requirements for compatibility, redundancy, inconsistency, emergent properties, and combined behaviors.

6.3.6.3 Ambiguity Tolerance

In traditional requirements engineering, tolerating ambiguity is a strategic measure intended to postpone specification of details until they are fully understood. In contrast, we expect uncertainty, ambiguity, and non-determinacy to be permanent characteristics of ULS systems. We therefore need research on the following:

Uncertain and Ambiguous Requirements. How do we best analyze, transform, and reason about requirements in the presence of uncertainty and ambiguity?

Requirements Drift. How do we represent and respond to ***requirements drift*** in socio-technical ecosystems where the presence of a new system can affect human and organizational dynamics, and therefore the requirements?

6.3.6.4 Requirements Phaseout

Traditional life-cycle models make provisions for a *phaseout* stage, during which a software system is phased out and replaced with a new system. The economics of ULS systems will be such that phaseouts will often be far in the future. We therefore need research on the following:

Life Cycle of Requirements. How do we provide for longevity by representing requirements in a way that accommodates the addition, deletion, modification, or recomposition of requirements over long periods of time and evolution?

6.3.7 Further Reading

Design in general, and the design of software and software-intensive systems in particular, is a topic that has received a great deal of study over many decades. Herbert Simon's epochal paper, "The Architecture of Complexity" (reprinted in his book, *The Sciences of the Artificial* [Simon 69]), provides a touchstone for significant thinking on the structure of complex systems, whether engineered or emergent. The basic idea is that for systems to be robust in the face of change, they must have a structure that is hierarchical or nearly so. Parnas's notion of information-hiding design modularity, first presented in his paper, "On the Criteria for Decomposing Systems into Modules" [Parnas 72], is an important prescriptive guideline to help developers design software that is robust to change. This idea reduces Simon's notion to an operational guideline for software engineers.

A separate but related stream of thinking emerged in the social sciences. Coase's famous paper, "The Nature of the Firm" [Coase 52], attempted to explain why the emergent structure of the capitalist economy is a collection of firms, not just one large firm. The question he tried to answer was roughly, "Why doesn't competition drive out all firms but one?" His answer revolved around concepts of transaction and organization costs driving the economy to a decentralized rather than a centralized structure. Carliss Baldwin and Kim Clark brought together these two lines of thinking in their book, *Design Rules: The Power of Modularity* [Baldwin 99]. In it, they try to account for the emergent, modular structure of the modern computer industry based on the idea that information-hiding modules in computer design create economic value in the form of real options (capital-investment analogs of financial options) and that the overall economy drives industry to organize itself to pursue this options value.

Boehm (for example in his book, *Software Engineering Economics* [Boehm 81] and in a more recent paper, "Software Economics: A Roadmap" [Boehm 00]) has pioneered the concept that software producers should optimize for value creation rather than merely for technical perfection.

Sullivan and colleagues [Sullivan 99] and Sullivan and Griswold and their students [Sullivan 01] have argued that concepts of real options, including the notions of Baldwin and Clark, can be operationalized to advance the theory and practice of software engineering. In particular, some recent work has shown that Baldwin and Clark's concept of design rules, as a formulation of what it means for a design to be modular, leads naturally to a generalized concept of interface. This concept can accommodate both an apparently non-hierarchical form of modularity being explored today under the rubric of aspect-oriented design [Griswold 06] and to the scaling up of software-based forms of modularity to the design of complex activities within firms and perhaps even to the structuring of industry sectors.

Any serious operationalization of this concept for ULS system design will require the precise formulation and validation of critical design rules. The work of Jackson [Jackson 06] on practical formal methods appears to hold significant promise to advance our capabilities in this dimension.

[Baldwin 99] Baldwin, C. & Clark, K. *Design Rules: The Power of Modularity.* Cambridge, MA: MIT Press, 1999.

[Boehm 81] Boehm, B. W. *Software Engineering Economics*. Prentice Hall, 1981.

[Boehm 00] Boehm, B. W. & Sullivan, K. "Software Economics: A Roadmap." *The Future of Software Engineering.* Association for Computing Machinery, 2000.

[Coase 52] Coase, R. H. "The Nature of the Firm." *Readings in Price Theory*. Stigler and Boulding (eds.). Chicago, IL: R. D. Irwin, 1952.

[Griswold 06] Griswold, W. G.; Sullivan, K.; Song, Y.; Shonle, M.; Tewari, N.; Cai, Y.; & Rajan, H. "Modular Software Design with Crosscutting Interfaces." *IEEE Software 23*, 1 (January/February, 2006): 51-60.

[Jackson 06] Jackson, D. *Software Abstractions: Logic, Language, and Analysis.* Cambridge, MA: MIT Press, 2006.

[Parnas 72] Parnas, D. L. "On the Criteria for Decomposing Systems into Modules." *Communications of the ACM 15*, 12 (December 1972):1053–1058.

[Simon 69] Simon, H. A. "The Architecture of Complexity," 192-229. *The Sciences of the Artificial.* Cambridge, MA: MIT Press, 1969.

[Sullivan 99] Sullivan, K. J.; Chalasani, P.; Jha, S.; & Sazawal, V. "Software Design as an Investment Activity: A Real Options Perspective." *Real Options and Business Strategy: Applications to Decision Making.* L. Trigeorgis (ed.). Risk Books, 1999.

[Sullivan 01] Sullivan, K.; Griswold, W. G.; Cai, Y; & Hallen, B. "The Structure and Value of Modularity in Software Design," 98-101. *Proceedings of the 8th European Software Engineering Conference,* held jointly with the 9th ACM SIGSOFT International Symposium on Foundations of Software Engineering, 2001.

6.4 Computational Engineering

To respond to rapidly changing environments, ULS systems will require fast and reliable component development and evolution. In addition, people with many different backgrounds and interests will need to understand quickly the design and operation of ULS systems and their components. To meet these needs, new approaches will be required to enable intellectual control at an entirely new level of scope and scale for analysis, design, and operation. Moreover, ULS systems will be defined and implemented in many languages, each with its own abstractions and semantic structures, creating requirements for analysis of artifacts in multiple semantic frameworks. Unfortunately, most existing programming languages treat software as an isolated, closed-world formal system. Such a view, although not without benefits, is not sufficient for the needs of ULS systems. We must evolve the capabilities of programming and other representational languages to make ULS systems more understandable at all levels of abstraction.

Another requirement is to create ULS systems out of larger and larger components. That is, if the granularity of reliable engineering artifacts can be scaled up sufficiently, the design, construction, and analysis of ULS systems will become more manageable. For example, a billion-line system becomes a million-unit system if the reliable unit of construction is a component of a thousand lines, and it becomes a ten- or hundred-unit system if hundred-thousand-line or ten-thousand-line subsystems, respectively, can be reliably built from reliable thousand-line components. Creating such large components and subsystems at the requisite level of reliability can be aided by computational analysis of software behavior that can be used to model, specify, verify, and test components as they are developed and evolved.

6.4.1 Expressive Representation Languages

Research Tracks

Essential

M2 (RT3)

M3 (RT5)

M3 (RT6)

To address these challenges, ULS systems will require increased language expressivity, an expanded view of ***abstraction***, and more powerful capabilities for modularity, ***composition***, ***verification***, and ***validation***. Abstraction mechanisms must be capable of spanning larger and more diverse kinds of phenomena, for example, very high-level specifications and architectures, error and exception propagation, quality-of-service management, nonfunctional characteristics, temporal properties, and ***crosscutting concerns***. More expressive ***domain-specific languages*** and models of architectural structures and computational dynamics will also be needed, as will design and code-generation capabilities based on these domain-specific models. Research will also be required in the areas of expressiveness, semantics, and modularity, including human comprehensibility and tradeoffs between expressiveness and comprehension, as described in the following subsections.

6.4.1.1 Improved Language Expressiveness

Improved languages are required for representing ULS systems and their components at all levels of abstraction. Today's languages focus largely on ***Von Neumann execution models*** rather than on policies, design rules, and specifications against which designs can be checked for conformance. Conceptual designs—as opposed to code-level designs—are rarely documented and not well supported by languages and associated tools. As a result, designs and their coded implementations often diverge, resulting in a loss of the semantic information and design rationale vital to their future evolution.

Many implementation faults originate from the difficulty of coding concepts that are clear and simple in the domain of the problem but unclear and complex when mapped to the domain of programming-language constructs. Today's languages are insufficient for ULS systems—they separate concerns poorly, are full of accidental complexities, are difficult to implement reliably, do not lend themselves adequately to analysis and optimization, and represent information in the solution domain rather than in the problem domain.

Promising research topics on language expressiveness include the following:

Domain-Specific Languages. Research is required to develop domain-specific language (DSL) semantics and syntax at all levels, from specification and architecture to design and implementation. This work will address new mechanisms for separating and viewing concerns, superimposition of multiple expressive views on code, representation of temporal relationships in domain terms rather than implementation terms, architectural and platform support for DSLs, automated synthesis of artifacts such as code from DSLs, generation of simulations and configuration descriptions from DSL models, and provision of language and support-system features that improve human learning and comprehension while reducing human errors.

Language Technologies for ULS System Development. Research is required in foundations of language design, including type-safe approaches to ***staged computation***, aspect-oriented composition of functional behavior and quality properties, representation of conceptual designs and their integration with code, and development environments for integrating nonlocal and legacy semantics and domain models with the semantics of newly developed artifacts. Technology development is also required to support loosely coupled interfaces between components (Jaron Lanier's ***phenotropics***[32] provide a good example) to simplify component composition. This work will also include exploration of new computational models and investigation of other disciplines such as biology for expressive models applicable to ULS systems.

Language Technologies for Human Communication. Research in language expressiveness will not be limited to the artificial elements of ULS systems, but will extend to people as well. This work will develop means for more effective human communication than is possible with today's graphical interfaces, including methods for sustained multi-party cross-organizational conversations during development and operation of ULS systems. Key objectives include language forms for reliable communication and understanding of policies, designs, and implementations, as well as real-time communication during system operation and evolution, all across widely varying stakeholder groups and environments.

6.4.1.2 Comprehensive Language Semantics

To enable computational methods for assessing behavior and quality attributes, ULS software engineering technologies can benefit from complete and correct definitions of the semantics of engineering languages and representations at all levels of exposition, from specifications and architectures to designs and implementations. Many important semantic relationships in software cross the program/non-program boundary. For example, identifiers in code relate to entities outside the code, and artifacts other than code define aspects of ULS systems at all levels of abstraction, including semantic references to code. These relationships may reference, for example, specifications, configuration files, build scripts, error databases, email archives of design discussions, etc. Research is thus needed in the following areas:

Foundations for ULS System Semantic Webs. Research will be required on technologies to support the rich semantic web among the intentional artifacts of ULS systems, including new and legacy specifications, designs, and code; simulations and models; domain-specific languages and programs; and many others. To keep pace with the perpetual evolution of ULS systems, these technologies will permit developers to reason about semantic webs to better understand the often nonlocal meaning of programs and other system representations.

32 See Brockman, John. *The Next Fifty Years: Science in the First Half of the Twenty-first Century.* Vintage, 2002.

Foundations for High-Level ULS System Abstractions. Research will be needed to develop frameworks and structures for abstract but precise representations of large-scale ULS system artifacts and to understand and support corresponding human methods of reasoning and analysis. Breakthroughs will be required in mathematical foundations for very high-level representations capable of supporting abstraction and refinement while preserving behavioral equivalence across widely varying levels of expression. Such abstractions must be mathematically sound, referentially transparent down to details, and low in complexity to enable intellectual control.

6.4.1.3 New Forms of Modularity

ULS systems will include many different stakeholders involved in defining and understanding both the modularity of ULS systems and the component compositions that the modularization implies. Research is needed in the following areas to support these objectives:

Modularization Views for Human Understanding. Research is required on foundations for view correspondence that will support multiple perspectives on ULS system modularizations and the relationships they imply. A promising approach is to develop a correspondence calculus that provides methods for assessing the difference between views and the abstractions they embody—for example, to determine if changing a view changes the system—and between different structural properties of views—for example, in assessing the hierarchical or ***crosscutting*** properties of various modularizations. Techniques will also be required to express and manipulate behaviors that do not modularize and compose along typical functional lines.

New Methods for Improved Modularization. Recent research has shown that it is possible to isolate and compose systems out of not just traditional block and hierarchical but also crosscutting structures. Moreover, work in biology and other disciplines suggests meaningful concepts of modularity that do not align with spatial co-location. To understand how functional and other requirements can be better allocated across components, this work will include investigation of artificially designed software and systems, such as digitally evolved analog circuits; robots and other devices designed by ***neuro-evolution***; and robots that employ ***probabilistic*** techniques and ***machine learning***. Biological systems such as the human immune system will be investigated to explore examples of non-monolithic modularity. In addition, generalized concepts of modularity based on design rules may transcend some limitations of traditional modularization concepts and permit a level of expressiveness required to accommodate crosscutting modularity.

6.4.2 Scaled-Up Specification, Verification, and Certification

Research Tracks

Essential	Support
M1 (RT2)	M2 (RT3)
M2 (RT4)	
M3 (RT5)	

As computational power increases, formal methods that might have once seemed intractable are becoming practical. Moreover, the engineering implications of formal foundations are becoming better understood. These trends provide an opportunity to harness computational power to help automate fundamental engineering operations in a next generation of more capable tools to support ULS system development.

6.4.2.1 Trusted Core Components

Because ULS systems will be highly decentralized and distributed, they will depend heavily on trusted core components throughout their architectures. These components include key operating system, middleware, and data-management components; communication protocols; and ***cryptographic*** implementations, all of which will participate in maintaining operational integrity across and within widely varying domains. These trusted core components, envisioned as small but essential portions of ULS systems, will participate in the coordination and integration of the majority of system components that may or may not be trusted. While complete specifications of ULS systems will likely be difficult to achieve, complete specifications of trusted components will be possible and necessary. Trusted cores will require complete specification to support correctness verification and ***certification***. Moreover, ULS systems will require trusted elements such as self-modifying and self-sustaining subsystems, adaptive control functions, and interacting autonomous agents. Developing technologies for achieving a sufficient level of ***trust*** in these elements will require research in the following area:

Specification, Verification, and Certification for Trustworthy ULS Systems. Research is needed for extending and scaling up theoretical foundations and engineering methods of existing specification techniques (for example, ***sequence-based specification*** and ***flow-structure analysis***); for defining precise semantics of specification languages, both for effective use and for development of automated support; and for verifying designs and implementations of trusted core components for correctness with respect to their specifications. Practical application of correctness verification on a broad scale requires research to scale up and automate existing methods (for example, ***function-theoretic verification***, ***proof-carrying code***, and ***model checking***). Research will also be required for certifying trusted components for fitness for use with scientific methods—for example, statistical, usage-based testing—to provide confidence that their implementations can be depended on to provide correct functionality in operational environments. Research is required to scale up these methods to certify the trusted components as well as to develop new methods for verifying and validating autonomous software components of ULS systems.

6.4.2.2 Cost-Effective Specification and Analysis

Complete, correct specifications of entire ULS systems and their subsystems may be difficult to achieve in practice. The properties on which participants depend, and which therefore must be specified, are open ended, and the cost of establishing required properties for every element of a ULS system may be prohibitive. What can be achieved in practice is a partial specification that grows as more information becomes available. The reliability of information in such partial specifications will vary; for example, it may arise from formal analysis, empirical data, or subjective judgment.

A key research question is thus how to validate ULS systems under these circumstances. If complete verification is impractical, how do participants decide how much of which validation activities are cost effective, and how do they determine whether the qualities of a ULS system are sufficient for its intended purpose? One approach is to develop an integrated framework for evolving specifications that supports partial and approximate knowledge, including

- specification of an open-ended set of properties;
- information about the level of trust in property values;
- analysis and validation techniques to assess the level of trust;
- estimation of the cost and value of analyses that produce new information; and
- propagation of new information for further analysis.

Research is thus required in the following area:

Sufficient Correctness for ULS Systems. New methods are required for drawing acceptably valid conclusions from incomplete, inconsistent, and changing knowledge about the system, its constituent parts, and the needs of its users. These methods involve both assessing the level of confidence in particular qualities for a class of tasks for a specific participant group and cost-effectively determining whether a ULS system in fact meets those qualities.

6.4.2.3 Model-Based Validation

Conventional development processes are based on assumptions of long life cycles with minimal requirements change and exhaustive test-case analyses. These processes are inadequate for ULS systems, particularly for the parts of the system that incur stringent quality-of-service requirements. We therefore need research in the following area:

Model-Based Validation for ULS Systems. Research is required on model-based methods to better understand their application to stringent certifiability and reliability requirements of ULS systems. For example, model-based formalisms are often amenable to verification for system correctness, and empirical benchmark generation enables certain performance properties to be verified. In addition, incorporating the models generated by requirements and specification languages into engineered development environments with improved human-computer interaction can facilitate use of formal methods while accounting for ease-of-use requirements.

6.4.3 Computational Engineering for Analysis and Design

Research Tracks

Essential

M1 (RT1)

M2 (RT3)

M2 (RT4)

M3 (RT5)

Software developers today lack practical means to determine and validate the full functional behavior of programs and their corresponding specifications, architectures, and designs. This shortcoming in present-day software engineering drives cost and complexity and will substantially inhibit development of ULS systems. Although computation of program behavior is a significant problem subject to theoretical limitations, engineering solutions are emerging—for example, in ***function-extraction*** technology—and we need to make progress in this area. Routine availability of computed behavior will substantially reduce the complexity and cost of software and system development, verification, and evolution.

> Computational Engineering for ULS System Analysis and Design

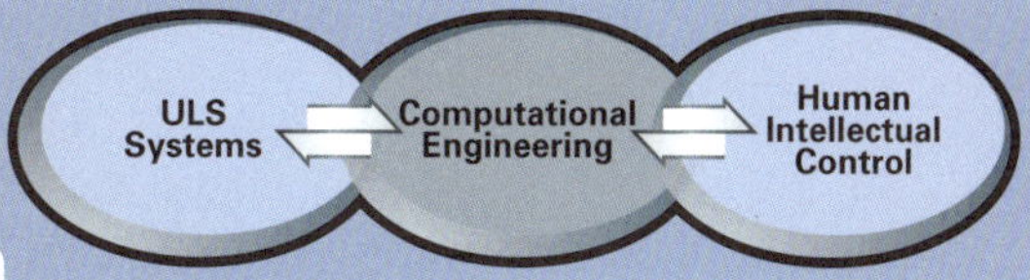

Relevance to DoD Missions

ULS systems must provide reliable mission capabilities to warfighters under adverse and unpredictable circumstances. The software will be depended on by many people, and so must be dependable. The task of developing dependable software at the scope and scale of ULS systems will exceed the capabilities of current software engineering methods that have evolved in the first 50 years of computing. A transformation to next-generation software engineering as a computational discipline will help augment human capabilities for fast and reliable development.

Key Concepts

Computational Engineering will encompass many technologies. For example, it will require automation to compute the behavior of software and other engineering artifacts, such as specifications and architectures, to the maximum extent possible for human intellectual control. This is an extremely difficult problem that will require innovative research. ***Function-theoretic foundations*** of software illuminate strategies for behavior computation based on the semantic structures of programming and other representation languages. The availability of computed behavior during system development and operation will help address problems of correctness verification, security analysis, and component composition as well.

We need the following research to enable computational automation for ULS system development and analysis:

Computation of Component Behavior in Development and Analysis. Component reliability requires that full functional behavior and quality attributes be known for validation against requirements and verification of correctness. Research is required on how to compute the behavior of software to the maximum extent possible. The objective is to replace current labor-intensive and error-prone analysis of program behavior in human-time scale with fast and correct computation of program behavior in CPU-time scale. This research can build on ***function-theoretic foundations***—for example, as found in ***cleanroom software engineering*** and function-extraction technology—that treat programs as rules for mathematical functions and relations. These foundations define procedure-free functional representations of program structures and algebraic methods for their derivation. Research will be needed in organizing and simplifying computed behavior expressions, as well as in the human factors of behavior presentation and analysis. Behavior computation can be expected to increase the span of human intellectual control and increase confidence in the correctness of software.

Computation of Component Compositions in Network Architectures. The overall behavior of compositions of components combined into network architectures must be calculated for fast and reliable system development and evolution. Composition computations must generate correct abstractions of the net behavior of combined components and further scale up the reliable unit of construction for ULS systems. Such a capability is important for developing and verifying the flow structures of enterprise tasks implemented through component compositions across distributed network architectures. Research can expand theoretical foundations and develop engineering automation for defining components in composable form and computing their composite behavior. This work can build on function-theoretic mathematical foundations that prescribe compositional methods for calculating the net behavior of combined components. We will also need research in specifying intercomponent domain representations suitable for compositional analysis.

Truth-Preserving Computation. ULS systems will require maintenance of correct self-descriptions of the structure and function of systems and components for both computational analysis and human intellectual control. Automated truth-maintenance capabilities can initially derive and subsequently preserve the correctness and completeness of these semantic descriptions as systems and their components change. We will need research to define semantics-based descriptions of systems and components and to develop computational methods both to preserve the truth of such descriptions under system evolution and to reveal violations of required behavioral invariances. Research will also be required to create a semantic calculus as a basis for truth-preservation computations.

6.4.4 Further Reading

A survey of methods and issues in developing domain-specific languages can be found in "When and how to develop domain-specific languages" by Mernik and colleagues [Mernik 05]. Neumann discusses development of trustworthy components and systems [Neumann 03] in terms of disciplined development processes, principle-driven architectures, and composable components. Prowell and colleagues provide background in function-theoretic methods for specification, verification, and certification [Prowell 99], and Pleszkoch and Linger [Pleszkoch 04] discuss technology for computational analysis of software behavior.

[Mernik 05] Mernik, M.; Heering, J.; & Sloane, A. "When and how to develop domain-specific languages." *ACM Computing Surveys 37*, 4 (2005): 316–344.

[Neumann 03] Neumann, P. *Principled Assuredly Trustworthy Composable Architectures* (SRI Project 11459, Final Report). Menlo Park, CA: Computer Science Laboratory, SRI International, June 28, 2003. http://www.csl.sri.com/neumann/chats4.html; also chats4.ps and chats4.pdf.

[Pleszkoch 04] Pleszkoch, M. & Linger, R. "Improving Network System Security with Function Extraction Technology for Automated Computation of Program Behavior." *Proceedings of the 37th Hawaii International Conference on System Sciences (HICSS-37),* Kona, HI. IEEE Computer Society Press, 2004.

[Prowell 99] Prowell, S.; Trammell, C. J.; Linger, R.; & Poore, J. H. *Cleanroom Software Engineering: Technology and Process*. SEI Series in Software Engineering. Reading, MA: Addison-Wesley Longman, 1999.

6.5 Adaptive System Infrastructure

Development environments provide an integrated set of languages and tools that aid the construction, integration, and validation of software artifacts and applications. The runtime infrastructure for executing applications is provided by deployment environments, such as networks, operating systems, and middleware. Today's software-development environments and deployment environments are heavily oriented toward traditional software-development practices that focus on the production and execution of software artifacts. They centralize activities in a single organization or with central points of control, as in traditional prime/subcontractor structures and open-source development.

ULS systems, in contrast, require an adaptive system infrastructure that supports the following:

- Integrated operation and evolution: Development, deployment, and operational activities will be more integrated and overlapping in ULS systems than in current practices, which are typically characterized by distinctions, such as the requirements phase, the design phase, and the testing phase. These distinctions between phases will be blurred or even lost in a ULS system.
- Decentralization: ULS systems will have many concurrent information flows among development, deployment, and operational activities and will be produced by decentralized design processes involving many participating organizations and be coordinated by architectural agreements.
- Design of all levels: ULS systems will require attention to production and operation as well as to engineering and management, which must be supported by an integrated development and operational environment. Engineering of ULS systems requires support for abstractions and views in order to manage the inherent complexity.
- Security and trust: Development and deployment that span organizational boundaries will require a system infrastructure that ensures the security and privacy of sensitive information and that manages continuously changing organizational boundaries.
- Continuous in situ evolution: Because of the blurring of the distinction between design time and runtime, ULS systems will increasingly be developed in situ, piecewise, in the operational environment. The number of changes will be so large that the ULS system cannot be treated as a monolithic system. Instead, deployment configurations will evolve, and changes will migrate through the ULS system.

The need to support an adaptive system infrastructure creates a need for research on decentralized production management, on view-based evolution of the system design, on evolutionary configuration and deployment in the operational environment, and on ***in situ control and adaptation*** of the operational system.

6.5.1 Decentralized Production Management

Research Tracks

Essential

M1 (RT1)

M3 (RT5)

M3 (RT6)

With a ULS architecture in place, companies and other organizations will be able to work in parallel to develop, select, deploy, and maintain system components. Environment support for system production and runtime management will, in many ways, resemble the support for software development provided by today's best software engineering tools and environments.

The production of ULS systems must be managed in a decentralized fashion across major boundaries (e.g., companies, countries, and even cultures). Because of legacy commitments and the wish to leverage technology advances, it is inevitable that a variety of development subenvironments and heterogeneous operational platforms will be used. Different firms and organizations will make different choices, and, in some cases, technology (e.g., specialized embedded processors, secure operating systems, and fault-tolerant middleware) will constrain developers' choices of language and tool environments as well as runtime platforms. Multi-team, multi-organization interoperability is critical to allow for the formation of ad hoc coalitions of companies into design teams.

The large-scale, distributed, decentralized—yet tightly coordinated—engineering activities that will be needed to develop and maintain ULS systems will require new approaches to multi-institution security.

Today's perimeter security paradigm dictates that integration across organizations generally happens outside of those organizations' firewalls, through the use of such mechanisms as demilitarized zones. Such methods will not scale economically to enable multi-organization development activities. In another dimension, development environments for ULS systems will themselves have to provide strict security control over the viewing of and access to design information and capabilities of running systems. In other words, as design information comes to be shared across teams and organizations while boundaries continually change, we will have to address ***trust*** and ***security*** of the intellectual properties as well as corporate and national security.

Without coordinated system integration and testing in otherwise desynchronized and decentralized design processes, users of ULS systems will have little confidence that their deployment configurations will operate as expected. To achieve such confidence, the following research is needed:

Multi-Team, Multi-Organization Interoperability. We will need research into an adaptive system infrastructure that combines development, deployment, and operational support for interoperability between deployment configurations and development and operational teams as well as between organizations to manage the development and operation of ULS systems. This interoperability research must address

- change control when design dependences span organizational boundaries;
- global analysis of systems under development when the components are developed across such boundaries;
- enforcement of development protocols across administrative domains (such as signoffs on software artifacts);
- contracting and accounting;
- mining of technical and social data across organizational boundaries (e.g., to find emergent or previously undocumented design dependencies or to map large-scale design structures);

- integrated support for economic analysis, contracting, and management-level monitoring and control;
- support for business intelligence and decision making;
- support for expressing and enforcing high-level development policies; and
- environment interfaces to regulatory/certification authorities.

Security and Trust. We need research to develop new models of security consistent with the need for much deeper, yet still secure, integration of information and activities across continually changing organizational boundaries. We also must be able to track the provenance of software and other design elements (for example, to track down all software produced by persons/organizations later found to have been tainted). Advances in security for development environments are likely to be applicable across many parts of ULS systems.

Coordinated System Integration and Testing. To ensure predictable operation of deployment configurations of ULS applications, the following issues must be addressed:

- supporting system integrators in their selection of components that emerge from ongoing competitions among suppliers;
- virtually integrated views of development activities that are distributed over many organizations, for purposes of early verification, problem detection, etc.
- system integration/build mechanisms taking inputs from across such boundaries; and
- support for automated and authenticated validation within and between domains and coalition partners.

6.5.2 View-Based Evolution

Research Tracks

Essential	Support
M2 (RT3)	M1 (RT2)
M2 (RT4)	M3 (RT6)

ULS systems and their designs will be extraordinarily complex and will thus be understandable only through abstract views that present the information essential to a task while eliding the bulk of irrelevant information and unnecessary detail. The concept of software and system views is not new. Advances in viewing and visualization technology, however, promise to ease software development and evolution tasks. Moreover, the unique characteristics of ULS systems create demanding new challenges, largely due to heterogeneity, decentralization, and complexity.

ULS systems will be too complex to treat as monolithic systems for purposes of system change. Rather, many changes will be made to ULS systems through *abstract views* that isolate those parts that are relevant to a given change. Integrated development environments and deployment environments could enable developers and operators to specify the applicability criteria for view-based modification policies and automatically apply them to all data flows, information flows, services, components, or events that satisfy the applicability criteria. What the environment does to effect such changes might be incomprehensible to the developers or operators, but the changes must be coherent and validated.

The following research is needed:

Abstract Views and Visualization. We need research leading to new development environments and deployment environments to enable developers to explore and visualize all manner of software artifacts and behaviors of ULS systems. Example artifacts and behaviors include requirements, design rules, code, executing behavior, hardware and network configurations, and load and performance characteristics. Development tools should be able to extract information from—and integrate across—artifacts in different languages, managed by different development and deployment environments, coming from separate hardware and software components, across company boundaries, from systems with dynamically changing network topologies, etc. Although much work has been and is going on in these areas, we need advances to address systems of immense scale that enable us to

- automatically produce views and the instrumentation required to update the set of defined views;
- include human state and behavior in technical system views;
- present parts of the system that are not designed by people to people in a comprehensible and usable form;
- visualize dependence structures among decisions in conceptual designs for the purposes of evaluating such properties as the likely cost of change or economic costs and benefits;
- determine the sorts of views that enable people to make *good* development/operation decisions; and
- determine how best to display or visualize the health of a ULS system to people (users, designers, and orchestrators) who are unable to comprehend the entire system.

Policy-Based Modifications. Research is needed to enable developers and operators to specify policies or criteria that future modifications of the system must satisfy and then support the enforcement of such policies. Enforcing policies can be difficult, perhaps requiring automated design and validation. Key research questions include the following:

- How are policies generated, specified, represented, enforced, and adapted over time?
- Are there changes to programming languages, computational models, development environments, or deployment environments that enable policy-based modifications?
- How is policy-based modification related to ***refactoring***?
- Can automated refactoring be used to accomplish some policy-based modifications?

6.5.3 Evolutionary Configuration and Deployment

Research Tracks

Essential	Support
M1 (RT1)	M3 (RT5)
M2 (RT3)	
M2 (RT4)	

Software engineers have traditionally created and configured entire applications internally and tested/released them into their deployment environments. In contrast, because of the blurring of the distinction between design time and runtime, ULS systems will increasingly be developed in situ in the deployment environment. This trend creates the need for synergistic development and deployment environments for deploying and configuring the behavior of reusable components to meet quality-of-service requirements in the context in which they execute. It also requires in situ systems, processes, and techniques for measurement, analysis, and modeling of the interactions among configuration choices and the achievement of desired functional and performance qualities.

Deployment configurations of ULS applications will use both trusted and untrusted components of the ULS system and operate in an environment that may include hostile components. Many such deployment configurations will be used in life-critical situations and require full trust of their users.

Development and deployment environments for ULS systems must support the capability for developers and operators to modify existing systems with new components, new versions of existing components, or alternative choices for configurable interfaces. Those modifications must be propagated consistently throughout deployment configurations.

Different deployment configurations will execute concurrently in the same operational ULS system. Component-version separation of co-resident deployment configurations, as well as stability of those configurations in light of the evolving ULS, will be critical to the robust operation of each deployment configuration.

Multiple component versions or deployment configurations will run simultaneously. Different deployment configurations must interoperate across different component versions to facilitate information interchange and to ensure robust operation through comparison of their outputs and effects. Instrumentation of the system to provide inputs to the multiple versions and monitor their outputs and effects must be automatically installed and inferred from the versions being monitored. These problems will be especially complicated because people and organizations will be parts of the ULS system. As a result, there is likely to be little chance for duplicating behavior from instance to instance.

Automatic rollover to new configurations, monitoring of the operations of these new configurations against expectations, and rollback to proven configurations are essential to a predictable operational environment.

We need research in the following topics for evolutionary configuration and deployment:

Trusted Deployment Configurations. Research is needed into mechanisms that maintain a desired degree of trustworthiness in deployment configurations during operation of the deployed configuration. Such mechanisms must exhibit a degree of resilience that is considerably higher than today's techniques deployed in today's Internet environment. Advances in security-and-trust technology for production management can be leveraged in this context.

Change Propagation in Deployment Configurations. Research is needed on how to analyze the effects of intended changes and how to propagate changes automatically and robustly into the set of known alternatives without negatively affecting system quality of service.

Deployment Configuration Co-Residence. Research is needed into mechanisms to enable developers and operators to isolate deployment configurations and detect interference between them.

Interoperability of Deployment Configurations. Research is needed into mechanisms to support interoperability in a multi-version environment and to enable developers and operators to detect, highlight, and comprehend functional and quality differences between simultaneous executions in the presence of non-artificial components.

Predictable System Rollover and Rollback. Research is needed into techniques to ensure that when rollback is required (e.g., due to a system malfunction that cannot be corrected by restarting one or more components), an earlier version of one or more components can be made available and a minimally disruptive consistent configuration can be deployed without negatively affecting system functionality and qualities.

6.5.4 In Situ Control and Adaptation

Research Tracks

Essential

(M1) (RT1)

(M1) (RT2)

(M2) (RT4)

(M3) (RT6)

ULS systems will have to respond to emergent behavior on the part of the users and the environment in which the system is situated. Consequently, the behavior of the system itself will be emergent. Existing systems use a manufacturing model: software is designed and constructed in a factory, and the completed software is deployed elsewhere. The design loop connects the field back to the factory—expert designers examine feedback from the field to produce subsequent versions. This design loop is too distant in time and space for ULS systems, which must provide continuous on-demand situational awareness and actuation capabilities to respond to emergent behaviors. These requirements create the need for mechanisms to facilitate manageable and safe in situ adaptation of ULS systems, so that ULS systems can be responsible for much of their evolution and so that human operation of the system, and hence errors caused by operator mistakes, can be minimized.

ULS systems must be able to observe their own operations (i.e., the operations of individual components, individual deployment configurations, and collections of deployment configurations), recognize acceptable and unacceptable behaviors, and take corrective action with little or no operator intervention. These adaptations must occur dependably to achieve a balanced level of quality for ULS system participants. Achieving these goals requires research into new capabilities for

- actively monitoring the activity of components and their environments;
- continually performing self-testing;
- detecting errors and automatically recovering from them;
- automatically configuring components during installation; and
- protecting the system from damage when patches and updates are installed as well as from attacks perpetrated against them during deployment and runtime.

Proposed research topics are the following:

Control-Theoretic Foundations for Adaptive Systems. A key challenge facing trustworthy adaptive ULS systems will be to develop models of system operation at the component, deployment-configuration, and system levels. Another key challenge will be to develop control algorithms that can ensure essential system-quality attributes while simultaneously handling rapidly changing demands and resource-availability profiles as well as varying service strategies and policies tuned for different environments. Control-theoretic techniques, in particular ***hybrid systems modeling***, involve algorithms and control mechanisms that handle rapidly changing demands and resource-availability profiles and configure these mechanisms with service strategies and policies tuned for different environments. Such control-theoretic models may have their roots in the control-systems domain or may be based on value-based quality-of-service models prevalent in the business domain. Research is therefore needed in scalable techniques and tools for developing controllers that can provide verifiable adaptation for ULS systems under a wide range of conditions in an automated manner. Such controllers must handle complex issues arising from the composition of adaptable components into collections of deployment configurations.

Decentralized Resource Management. Because of the decentralized and distributed nature of ULS systems, it will not be feasible to know the entire set of application tasks that will run, the loads they will impose on system resources in response to dynamically changing environments, or the order in which the tasks will execute. This dynamism can occur because the number of combinations in which application tasks can be mapped to system resources is too large to compute efficiently or because task runtime behaviors are simply too variable to predict accurately. Research is therefore needed in decentralized resource-management algorithms and mechanisms that can robustly optimize system responses to changing environments or requirements, such as changing component interconnections, power levels, CPU/network bandwidth, ***latency/jitter,*** and dependability needs. Such algorithms must ensure the operational safety and correct functioning of the ULS system viewed as a control system (e.g., control model validation and certification) and calibrate the ULS control system to improve performance and adjust to changes over time.

Predictable Reconfiguration. We envision that ULS system participants will develop, test, and operate new deployment configurations and reconfigurations in operational systems, and that these systems will have to simultaneously manage component versions and deployment configurations based on automated observations and rules of acceptable behavior. The adaptations of ULS systems must be coordinated with the desire of ULS system users to evolve and adapt their deployment configurations. Research is therefore needed in techniques that coordinate and resolve the conflict between the desire for ULS systems to operate and optimize their behavior autonomously and the need for users to believe that they are in control of their operating environments (i.e., to predictably evolve their system configurations).

Transparent Reflection. ***Reflection*** makes the internal organization of ULS systems both visible and changeable for system-infrastructure and application software to inspect and modify at runtime. Research is therefore needed in robust mechanisms for supporting such reflection without unduly degrading quality of service or obscuring the application architecture of deployment configurations from users. In other words, runtime monitoring, feedback, and transition mechanisms (e.g., dynamic reconfiguration or online recompilation) are needed to change application and system behavior robustly (e.g., while meeting stringent end-to-end robustness requirements) without changing the basic implementation structure of applications.

Similarly, mechanisms are needed to support decentralized and distributed data collection and data fusion based on incomplete and approximate data.

Policy-Driven Migration Management. Different users of the ULS system will evolve their deployment configurations according to their own needs and interests. In that process, they will utilize components available as part of the ULS system infrastructure or provided by the ULS component marketplace. They will expect to be in control of the evolution of their deployment configurations. However, at times it will be essential that ULS system users migrate their deployment configurations to new versions of components—in particular, new versions of components that may have been compromised, that place undue resource constraints on the ULS system, and that critically affect the operation of other components. Research is needed into mechanisms that achieve such policy-driven migration without unduly restricting the freedom of ULS system users and without becoming a tool that can be misused for unauthorized forced migration to vulnerable system-component variants.

6.5.5 Further Reading

Raymond's *The Cathedral & the Bazaar: Musings on Linux and Open Source by an Accidental Revolutionary* [Raymond 01] is a comprehensive treatment of the open-source movement, which is our best example of decentralized production management. Kruchten [Kruchten 95] provides an overview of architectural views and how each of them can be used to achieve engineering control over a different set of system qualities and concerns. Subramonian [Subramonian 04] and Mikic-Rakic [Mikic-Rakic 05] and their colleagues discuss configuration, deployment, and redeployment considerations. Finally, two recent papers by Ye [Ye 05] and Wang [Wang 05] and their colleagues address ***in situ control and adaptation*** by providing schemes for managing reliability and performance via middleware.

[Kruchten 95] Kruchten, P. "The 4+1 View Model of Architecture." *IEEE Software 12*, 6 (1995): 42–50.

[Mikic-Rakic 05] Mikic-Rakic, M.; Malek, S.; & Medvidovic, N. "Improving Availability in Large, Distributed Component-Based Systems Via Redeployment." *Proceedings of the 3rd International Working Conference on Component Deployment*. Grenoble, France, November 28-29, 2005.

[Raymond 01] Raymond, E. *The Cathedral & the Bazaar: Musings on Linux and Open Source by an Accidental Revolutionary*. O'Reilly, 2001.

[Subramonian 04] Subramonian, V.; Shen, L-J; Gill, C.; & Wang, N. "The Design and Performance of Dynamic and Static Configuration Mechanisms in Component Middleware for Distributed Real-Time and Embedded Systems." *Proceedings of the 25th IEEE International Real-Time Systems Symposium*. Lisbon, Portugal, December 5-8, 2004.

[Wang 05] Wang, X.; Lu, C.; & Koutsoukos, X. "Enhancing the Robustness of Distributed Real-Time Middleware via End-to-End Utilization Control." *IEEE Real-Time Systems Symposium (RTSS '05)*, December 2005.

[Ye 04] Ye, J.; Loyall, J.; Shapiro, R.; Schantz, R.; Neema, S.; Abdelwahed, S.; Mahadevan, N.; Koets, M.; & Varner, D. "A Model-Based Approach to Designing QoS Adaptive Applications." *25th IEEE International Real-Time Systems Symposium*. Lisbon, Portugal, December 5-8, 2004.

6.6 Adaptable and Predictable System Quality

ULS systems will be long running and must operate robustly in environments fraught with failures, overloads, and attacks. Moreover, ULS systems must maintain robustness in the presence of adaptations that are not centrally controlled or authorized and that, in some cases, may be initiated by the systems themselves.

At ultra-large scale, new kinds of system behavior, and therefore new ***quality attributes***, may arise. For example, ***Internet storms*** arise at the massive scale of the Internet but do not appear in smaller scale settings. Predicting and averting these types of phenomena require novel theories and applications of approaches inspired by such fields as ***statistical mechanics*** and ***possibility theory***.

Predicting and preserving system-wide qualities requires establishing and sustaining the system invariants on which these qualities depend. A variety of enforcement mechanisms have been developed over many years of practice (for example, transaction monitors, security monitors, sandboxes, and schedulers, to name a few). We must establish whether these enforcement mechanisms are suitable at ultra-large scale and must find new, more suitable mechanisms where necessary. Moreover, enforcement mechanisms must be designed both to accommodate an incipient level of hardware and software failure that is inevitable in ULS systems and to provide graceful behavior degradation and recovery in the presence of failures.

Some degree of system failures (hardware and software) will be as intrinsic to ULS systems; for example, at any given moment, some portion of the Internet is in failure mode. It is inevitable that ULS systems will be inviting targets of attack for capable and motivated adversaries seeking tactical and strategic advantages. Although attacks do not fall under the purview of typical quality-of-service concerns, there is an obvious correlation between the treatment of vulnerabilities and the treatment of other system qualities that are frequent targets of attack.

Because of the significant human element in ULS systems, quality attributes will apply to the human and organizational components as well as to hardware and software components. On the one hand, a more comprehensive treatment of human factors in immersive and ***ubiquitous computing*** systems is required. On the other hand, correlations between human behavior and traditional system quality attributes will become more prominent. For example, the reliability of one part of a ULS system might depend on human coordination among multiple organizations.

Engineering management is another facet of the human element that must be revisited for systems at ultra-large scale. Developing practices that foster continuous product and process improvement across organizational boundaries is just one of many challenges confronting engineering management at ultra-large scales. Moreover, new product and process measures and new technical infrastructures will be required to support management decision making.

6.6.1 Robustness, Adaptation, and Quality Attributes

Research Tracks

Essential	Support
M1 **(RT2)**	M1 (RT1)
M2 **(RT4)**	M3 (RT5)

Dynamic systems in general are quasi-stable around a defined number of system states[33] that correspond to (possibly unbounded) regions of observable system behavior. In the systems context, ***robustness*** can be thought of as the tendency of a system to remain within a specified state space (i.e., a region) even in the presence of perturbations of one or more control variables. Analogously, systems large and small must maintain ***quasi-stability*** with respect to required qualities of service, and in these cases, robustness can be thought about in terms of traditional quality-attribute specifications. For example, reliability, safety, and availability can be specified in terms of the probability that a system will be in or remain in a specific state for some period of time. This form of requirement specification is widely seen in practice, regardless of whether there are sufficiently robust quality-attribute theories to ensure such qualities analytically.

Achieving robustness in ULS systems poses unique challenges not only in terms of the quasi-stability of system functions in the sense we have described, but also in terms of the system's quasi-stability under the effects of evolutionary pressure. A ULS system will likely have no single point of authority for version control and changes in system configuration, including the release of new software components or versions of components, new hardware and network technology, and new interconnections between systems and components. These changes may be individually small and, therefore, may not disrupt the quasi-stability of the ULS system. However, the accumulating weight of successive evolutionary steps may result in fundamental discontinuities (or ***phase transitions***) in system behavior.

33 This is a result of ***self-organizing criticality***. Open, ***dissipative systems*** typically gravitate toward an equilibrium that is not a true stable point (quasi-stability or ***metastability***)—because conditions are always changing (the openness of the system means that things are being put into it, while the system dissipates those things).

Analogies to this phenomenon arise frequently in the physical sciences. One illustration is the stability of sand piles. Dropping a single grain of sand on the sand pile will, in most cases, have little effect. Occasionally, however, a single grain of sand will produce an avalanche—a phase transition—from the old sand pile that has become unstable under accumulated change to the new sand pile. This phenomenon is widely encountered in physical systems (e.g., percolation, ***annealing***, and states of matter).

We need theories of robustness along with supporting mechanisms that accommodate both the traditional concepts of instantaneous robustness and the time-sequenced concept of robustness that arises from the decentralized, adaptive, and long-lived nature of ULS systems. To develop such theories, we need research on the following topics:

Signals for Robustness Limits. Is the sand pile less robust just before an avalanche than it is immediately after an avalanche? There are results from ***complexity science*** that suggest that there may be universal laws that operate on natural *and* artificial systems. Research here will seek to uncover signals in development processes (e.g., numbers of reported adaptations) and runtime processes (e.g., system dynamics) that predict impending phase transitions and determine the extent to which these signals depend on particular quality attributes.

Natural Systems Robustness. A study of natural robustness is an essential adjunct to the characterization of a ULS system as an ecosystem. Naturally occurring systems such as the human autonomic system and natural habitats achieve robustness in the face of change through feedback, filtering, self-repair, adaptation, and flexibility at many levels of abstraction. The study of mechanisms arising in naturally robust systems, where robustness emerges from the interaction of many complementary mechanisms, may suggest new mechanisms or combinations of existing, possibly revised mechanisms that would help make ULS systems robust.

6.6.2 Scale and Composition of Quality Attributes

Research Tracks

Essential

M3 (RT6)

Two fundamental strategies for dealing with scale and scale-induced complexity are ***abstraction*** and (de)***composition***. Abstraction seeks to hide irrelevant details; composition seeks to divide and conquer.

Not all phenomena readily admit to both strategies; for example, models of system behavior governed by shared-resource use (e.g., performance governed by shared CPU) typically abstract many details not pertaining to time, but these same theories tend not to be strictly compositional. In this case, the potentially adverse effect of non-compositionality on the computability of system quality is moderated by the use of abstraction. On the other hand, abstraction may give rise to non-determinacy. Non-determinacy is accommodated through the use of statistical techniques; we sacrifice the ability to predict a single event in favor of predicting the aggregate behavior of many events.

This is a recapitulation of an argument in the ULS system context that is well established in the physical sciences: *more is different*. That is, although phenomena at one level of system organization may be able to be (and indeed, are expected to be) derived from phenomena at a lower level of organization, higher level models are nevertheless appropriate. For example, the ideal gas laws are statistical mechanical (***stochastic***) descriptions of particle-level phenomena that can also be described deterministically at a more primitive but usually computationally intractable level of description.

Some phenomena, however, are not susceptible to either abstraction or composition—for example, high-dimension control theories that exhibit chaotic behavior (e.g., atmospheric phenomena and market phenomena). New computational theories may be needed to analyze or simulate these effects in ULS systems, for example to predict or simulate and control the effects of Internet storms or their equivalent in high-demand ad-hoc networks in the future battlespace.

Research is therefore needed on the following topics:

Complementary Stochastic and Deterministic Theories of System Quality. The repertoire of complementary—***deterministic*** and stochastic—quality-attribute theories must be expanded and enriched. Such theories exist in a limited form for timing but must be extended to other quality attributes such as security and availability. This research must address mutual quality-attribute dependencies and effects and enable combined quality claims across components of the system, overlapping subsystems, and enforcement mechanisms.

Verification with Aleatoric Uncertainty. Verification technology has traditionally been reduced to (dis)proving assertions about system behavior, or more particularly about the correspondence of an implementation to its specification. Recent advances in fully automated verification, for example in software ***model checking***, are encouraging but must be extended to accommodate ***aleatoric*** uncertainty, in particular uncertainty arising from non-determinism and measurement error. Possibilities include research in verification using ***multi-valued logics***, ***belief logics***, and analogous model logics.

Analysis and Verification with Epistemic Uncertainty. ***Epistemic uncertainty*** arises due to a lack of knowledge; it is wholly distinct from uncertainty that arises from aleatoric uncertainty, which arises from non-determinism and the measurement error. As systems increase in scale, our knowledge about the behavior of any of their parts will diminish, and what we may know may be out of date and therefore incorrect at the time this information will be used. Research on ***evidence theory*** (e.g., ***Dempster-Shafer theory***), ***possibility theory*** (e.g., ***fuzzy sets***), and related fields is needed.

6.6.3 Understanding People-Centric Quality Attributes

Research Tracks

Essential	Support
(M1) (RT1)	(M2) (RT3)
(M1) (RT2)	(M3) (RT6)
(M3) (RT5)	

People are part of a ULS system. The overall quality attributes of the system include quality attributes of the human parts as well as the artificial parts, and the interactions between the two. Therefore we need research on the following topics:

Trustworthy People-Comprehensible Models of System State. We need to understand how to develop accurate models of the system *that humans can trust*, so that they can react appropriately. Often human errors in existing systems can be traced to the fact that people either are not informed about underlying problems in the system (e.g., the Chernobyl disaster, the 2003 North American blackout); were informed about system state, but it was incorrectly reported (e.g., the Three Mile Island disaster); or did not believe what the system was reporting to them about its internal state.

Modeling People-People Interactions. Part of the failure of the North American power grid in 2003 can be traced to the fact that operators in Parma, Ohio did not notify operators in neighboring regions about troubles in their own power grid. Similarly, air traffic accidents are often related to miscommunications or mishandled interactions among people. Since people are an integral part of a ULS system, their mental state and the nature of their reactions, particularly in stressful circumstances, must be modeled so that the system can be designed appropriately and can react appropriately during operation. Thus research is required on creating models of human-human interaction. This research is related to the topics discussed in Section 6.1 on human interaction.

Modeling Human Quality Attributes. As integral parts of a ULS system, human performance, human reliability, and human security, to name just three examples, will affect *system* performance, availability, and security. While the human aspect in security has been long recognized, we seldom model human performance or reliability when we design systems. Some models of human performance do exist, but they focus on human performance in highly structured, repetitive tasks (e.g., operator performance in a directory-assistance task). Research is needed to broaden the scope of such models and to include other quality attributes such as reliability. This research must also integrate system-oriented measures of quality attributes with human-oriented measures. In addition, research is needed on designing human protocols and interactions within the system so that a desired state of performance, reliability, safety, etc. can be achieved. For example, in air traffic control, human redundancy is employed to ensure that no single failure of a human is catastrophic for the system's performance, reliability, or safety.

Modeling Crowd Behavior. While research exists on modeling individual people in their interactions with a system, there is a need for research in the social psychology of crowds. For example, many web-site crashes have been attributed to the sites being too popular (e.g., a web site selling tickets to a popular concert) and not to any nefarious intent by an adversary. Since ULS systems are ecosystems, the behaviors of the people within the system will greatly affect the state of the system, potentially causing worst-case behaviors to emerge. Research is needed, then, to model the use of ULS systems crowds in order to determine worst-case usage scenarios for performance, reliability, and security. Since people are rational actors, this research is related to the discussion of algorithmic mechanism design found in Section 6.2.1.

Blending Human and System Quality Attributes. Given that a ULS system depends on the behavior of both the human and the computational elements, research is needed that blends traditional quality-attribute models with human quality-attribute models, discussed above, to determine how these elements should be combined. Research questions include

- Should the computational part of the system respond when the human components fall below certain thresholds?
- How should the human part of the system respond when the artificial part falls below certain thresholds?
- Are there ways for each part to compensate for the other or help the other maintain good levels?

6.6.4 Enforcing Quality Requirements

Research Tracks

Essential	Support
M1 (RT1)	M2 (RT3)
M1 (RT2)	M2 (RT4)
M3 (RT6)	

Every theory makes assumptions about its environment. For quality attributes, some of these assumptions can be discharged by particular runtime enforcement mechanisms. There are a number of well-known quality-enforcement mechanisms today for timing, reliability, transactions, security, and so forth. In some cases, we need research to scale them to ULS system scale; in other cases, completely new mechanisms are needed. In all cases, the enforcement mechanisms must be linked explicitly with the complementary quality theories. Topics of particular research interest for enforcing quality requirements include the following:

Enforcement Mechanisms for Shared Resources. Many quality attributes are affected by policies for managing scarce, shared resources. Reservation and admission-control mechanisms are examples of well-known mechanisms that must be enhanced to address issues of scale and trust in ULS systems. In addition, these mechanisms must be parameterized to enforce or adapt to new attribute-theory-specific invariants.

Recovery-Oriented Computing. Because system failures and human errors are inevitable, we must focus attention on providing ULS systems that can recover from errors and operate through attacks rather than shut down completely. For example, we need robust mechanisms to ensure the necessary degree of replication to guard against partial system failures and attacks or to provide guaranteed, best-effort, conditional, or statistical levels of quality of service in the face of failure.

Acceptability-Oriented Computing. Reliably providing increasingly complex functionality may not be possible in ULS systems because the limitations of our abilities to design and implement correctly have been surpassed. In these cases, there may be approaches that will enable the construction of computer systems that can sustain (potentially self-inflicted) damage, process unexpected or illegal inputs, and take incorrect actions, yet nevertheless continue to execute productively.

6.6.5 Security, Trust, and Resiliency

Research Tracks

Essential	Support
M1 (RT2)	M1 (RT1)
M2 (RT4)	M3 (RT6)
M3 (RT5)	

We currently have difficulty achieving high levels of security even with state-of-the-art ***systems of systems***. For ULS systems, we will need security, trust, and resiliency to be at an acceptably high, measurable level so that users can trust that these systems will reliably achieve their objectives. ***Security*** is the capability of the system to provide confidentiality, integrity, and availability on the ULS system data and services both locally and globally. ***Trust*** is the extent to which users of the ULS system will be able to rely on the data and services of the ULS system. ***Resiliency*** is the capability of the ULS system to maintain an acceptable level of service while under stress from adverse environmental conditions such as attacks or cascading failures.

While we have an extensive history of research in the area of system security, the results of this research to date apply only to the small-system or component level of systems. We will need to apply these qualities to all levels of the ULS system including the creation, acquisition, deployment, integration, and operation of the system. Significant automation in the detection and response to threats to the ULS system will be a necessary component: the system will be too complex for any analyst to realize the ultimate effect of the multitude of simultaneous attacks and failures continuously experienced by the ULS system. As the systems become integrated with a dynamic arrangement of coalition partners and participants, the separation between external attackers and insider attackers will also be blurred.

Standard enforcement mechanisms and design approaches to achieve a given level of service are generally not designed to detect attacks.[34] At best, they are conceived to deliver certain kinds and levels of functionality in the presence of disturbances. Unfortunately, many such mechanisms may actually provide an attack mechanism with the routes it needs to be able to spread. In some cases, the correct approach to an attack is to violate quality guarantees for the sake of preserving other, more important, parts of the system.

34 The information that these mechanisms and approaches happen to collect in the process of dealing with failures may be useful for detecting an attack.

Research is required in the following areas:

Security, Trust, and Resiliency Measures and Metrics. We currently have no measures or metrics for security, trust, or resiliency that apply to our envisioned ULS systems. It may be possible to obtain useable measures for ULS systems using a statistical approach, much like statistical thermodynamics provides important measures for particle dynamics in the aggregate.

Attack Detection. Detecting attacks is distinct from detecting failures or providing service at some guaranteed levels. Perhaps detecting attacks requires active mechanisms similar to immune systems. We should investigate the possibility that ***machine learning*** could be used to detect attack-based anomalies.

Attack Containment. Containing attacks might involve cordoning off parts of the system and permitting only very carefully screened communications between the possibly attacked parts and the rest. This would require communication mechanisms optimized for safety and caution rather than efficiency.

Graceful Degradation Under Attack. Degrading gracefully might require dropping below service guarantees. Reflection might be required to pause some of the ULS system's operations while the system assesses itself and plans how to proceed.

Recovering from Attacks. How can the system repair itself after an attack (or bad failure of some sort)? Is checkpointing practical? Should components be required to be able to restart/reinitialize themselves? Can specifications play a role?

Attack Diagnostics and Forensics. Diagnosing attacks might require the ULS system to have a model of itself against which it can check. Perhaps testing code developed during development can be used; perhaps self-descriptions can be created using immunological or statistical means.

6.6.6 Engineering Management at Ultra-Large Scales

Research Tracks

Essential	Support
M2 **(RT3)**	M1 (RT2)
M2 **(RT4)**	M3 (RT5)

Because of the unprecedented scale of ULS systems, quality must be a paramount concern. Proper system performance will require the cooperative interaction of reasonably large portions of these systems. Therefore, the defect content of their parts must be kept low enough so that their testing can be completed in a reasonable time period and so that they can be maintained in proper operation for reasonably long periods of time. This calls for a consistently high level of quality work on the part of the developers, enhancers, and maintainers of all aspects of ULS systems.

To ensure high-quality work throughout such systems, quality-management guidelines and measurement frameworks are required that can identify poor-quality work and direct management attention to the sources of problems. Quality work is done only by people who strive to produce quality results. Because much of the design, development, and maintenance work on ULS systems will be knowledge work, and because the quality of knowledge work is largely controlled by the knowledge workers themselves, means to motivate quality work are needed together with means to measure and identify quality deviations without demotivating the knowledge workers. Research is needed, therefore, in the following areas:

Motivating and Managing the ULS System Knowledge Worker. Significant research at the boundaries of technology, management, and psychology is needed to discover methods to track work so that both poor- and good-quality work can be attributed to people and organizations without demotivating individual knowledge workers or producing perverse organizational competition.

Measurements of System and Process, Product, and Project Health. The quality of engineering management decisions depends on judgment and data. While measures of software quality and program status have been developed over many years of painful experience, new orders of scale present new challenges. Research is needed in measures for ULS systems that are akin to those used at the gross scale of ***econometrics*** (for example, the discovery of *leading indicators* for ***system health)*** and in techniques to sample this data across various organizational, contractual, social, technical, and temporal boundaries.

6.6.7 Further Reading

The references cited in Section 6.1.6 focus primarily on understanding people-centered design, human behavior, and ***context-aware computing***. In this section, we are more concerned with people as information processors—their inputs, outputs, and processing capabilities. Models of human performance in human-computer interaction have existed and been experimentally validated for decades. Some of the classic works in this area are those of Card, Newell, Kieras and others [e.g., Card 83, Elkind 90, Kieras 88]. Studies on the behavior of crowds can be found in *Collective Behavior* by Turner & Killian [Turner 93].

Although a bit dated with regard to technology, the issues raised in the National Research Council report *Trust in Cyberspace* [Schneider 98] still outline the important security characteristics—characteristics that will be even more problematic in the context of ULS systems. The work on information survivability, started by the Defense Advanced Research Projects Agency (DARPA) in 1994 and continuing through 2001 is well represented by Moore and colleagues [Moore 01] and by Kyamakya and colleagues [Kyamakya 00]. The latter work extended the security concept to systems of systems and, while still not sufficient for ULS systems, provides a base on which to build. Finally for attack recognition, the seminal paper by D. Denning [Denning 87] is still the best reference available for framing the issues involved in distributed attack detection.

Patterson, Fox, and their colleagues have researched techniques for monitoring and correcting execution [Patterson 02, Candea 01, Candea 04]. Rinard and his students and colleagues are studying how to make the execution of systems more robust by detecting data-structure corruption and repairing it [Rinard 03, Rinard 05]. Further, they are investigating when errors and failures can be tolerated during execution and exactly how to proceed effectively with execution after an error or failure.

[Candea 01] Candea, G. & Fox, A. "Recursive Restartability: Turning the Reboot Sledgehammer into a Scalpel." *Proceedings of the 8th Workshop on Hot Topics in Operating Systems (HotOS-VIII)*. Schloss Elmau, Germany, May 2001.

[Candea 04] Candea, G.; Brown, A.; Fox, A.; & Patterson, D. "Recovery Oriented Computing: Building Multi-Tier Dependability." *IEEE Computer 37*, 11 (Nov. 2004).

[Card 83] Card, S.; Moran, T.; & Newell, A. *The Psychology of Human-Computer Interaction.* Hillsdale, NJ: Lawrence Erlbaum Associates, 1983.

[Denning 87] Denning, D. "An Intrusion-Detection Model." *IEEE Transactions on Software Engineering 13*, 2 (Feb. 1987): 222-232.

[Elkind 90] Elkind, J.; Card, S.; Hochberg, J.; & Huey, B. (eds.). *Human Performance Models for Computer Aided Engineering.* San Diego, CA: Academic Press, Inc., 1990.

[Kieras 88] Kieras, D. E. "Towards a practical GOMS model methodology for user interface design." *The Handbook of Human-Computer Interaction.* Helander, M. (ed.). Amsterdam: North-Holland Elsevier, 1988.

[Kyamakya 00] Kyamakya, K.; Jobmann, K.; & Meincke, M. "Security and Survivability of Distributed Systems: An Overview," *IEEE MILCOM 2000*, Los Angeles, CA, 2000.

[Moore 01] Moore, A.; Ellison, R.; & Linger, R. *Attack Modeling for Information Security and Survivability* (CMU/SEI-2001-TN-001, ADA388771), Pittsburgh, PA: Software Engineering Institute, Carnegie Mellon University, 2001.

[Patterson 02] Patterson, D.; Brown, A.; Broadwell, P.; Candea, G.; Chen, M.; Cutler, J.; Enriquez, P.; Fox, A.; Kiciman, E.; Merzbacher, M.; Oppenheimer, D.; Sastry, N.; Tetzlaff, W.; Traupman, J.; & Treuhaft, N. *Recovery-Oriented Computing (ROC): Motivation, Definition, Techniques, and Case Studies* (UCB CSD-02-1175). Berkeley, CA: University of California, Berkeley, 2002.

[Rinard 03] Rinard, M. "Automatic Detection and Repair of Errors in Data Structures," 221–239. *Companion to the 18th Annual ACM SIGPLAN Conference on Object Oriented Programming, Systems, Languages, and Applications*, Anaheim, CA, October 26–30, 2003.

[Rinard 05] Rinard, M.; Cadar, C.; & Nguyen, H. H. "Exploring the Acceptability Envelope." *Companion to the 20th Annual ACM SIGPLAN Conference on Object-Oriented Programming, Systems, Languages, and Applications*. San Diego, CA, October 16–20, 2005.

[Schneider 98] Schneider, F. (ed.). *Trust in Cyberspace*. Washington, DC: National Academy Press, 1998.

[Turner 93] Turner, R. & Killian, L. *Collective Behavior,* 4th edition. Englewood Cliffs, NJ: Prentice Hall, 1993.

6.7 Policy, Acquisition, and Management

ULS systems will be developed to support national priorities and enable the missions they define. The systems will require rapid development and evolution to keep pace with changing mission objectives. To achieve this requirement, capability for fast and flexible adaptation must be built in as a first-class functional property of ULS systems and their supporting ecosystems. The systems must be explicitly designed to accommodate change at all levels, and their acquisition processes must be designed to support dynamic changes in system capabilities. Slow-paced processes for policy definition, system acquisition, and program management will be insufficient for this purpose. Fast acquisition will require fundamental changes in processes that are not well suited to acquiring software, where the possibility for rapid response exists but is largely unrealized. Acquisition for ULS systems will be highly distributed, ranging from planned development of strategic system capabilities to opportunistic incorporation of components in the field to meet immediate tactical needs. It is important to note that the acquisition processes and their supply chains should be regarded not as separate entities, but rather as first-class components of ULS ecosystems, subject to the same attention to design and evolution as operational software components.

ULS systems will present problems in management and coordination that must remain tractable as scale increases. The people and organizations in ULS systems will have different, time-varying, and often competitive or even adversarial objectives. Moreover, the actions of particular individuals and organizations may affect the ability of others to accomplish their goals, and the success of one group may depend on appropriate actions by other groups. This kind of situation is often referred to as a ***wicked problem***.

More generally, ULS systems will encompass the actions of all system participants, including not only computational elements but also human developers, administrators, operators, and users. Even if participants operate in good faith, it may be difficult for them to understand the full context and implications of their actions. Policy and management frameworks for ULS systems must therefore address both global constraints and local freedom of action. Organizational, technical, and operational policies and rules at all levels must be developed and largely automated to enable fast and effective local actions while preserving global capabilities.

6.7.1 Policy Definition for ULS Systems

Research Tracks

Essential	Support
M3 (RT5)	M1 (RT2)
M3 (RT6)	

Given the scope and scale of ULS systems, technical, organizational, and operational policies will emerge as principal vehicles for ensuring harmonious operations at all levels. Conformance to policies will become the price of entry for participation in ULS systems, and fast assessment of policy conformance will become critically important.

In terms of policy formulation, competition can arise among participants in ULS systems even if that is not their intention. Policies must support both local and global operations in such a way that people and the computational actions they initiate can achieve cooperative and even competing objectives without impairing the viability of the system as a whole. For example, because some tasks will be more urgent than others and because preserving overall functionality may be more important than providing ideal service under all circumstances, not everyone will experience the same quality of service. Such considerations require definition of policies whose effect on system operations, stability, and long-term viability is well defined and widely understood. Because of the central role of policy in ULS systems, research is required on the following topics:

Policy Definition for Flexible Collaboration. ULS system policies will have to reconcile diverse and competing objectives while providing complete and unambiguous semantic content sufficient to govern distributed-system development, evolution, and operation. Policy makers will have to deal with multiple stakeholders whose objectives are often incompatible and poorly articulated. Policy definition in such environments would be slow and laborious. Research is required to develop more effective processes for definition and use of content-rich policies as a first-class mechanism for achieving long-term sustainability of ULS socio-technical ecosystems. These processes must address conflict resolution, encourage flexible collaboration, and build consensus on an unprecedented scale, as well as provide closed-loop feedback mechanisms for incorporating improvements. They must be both system-centric for preserving global viability and user-centric for incorporating local policies, adaptations, and innovations.

Policy Content for Effective Governance. Research is required in how to define ULS system policies that specify organizational, technical, and operational constraints for global system integrity and freedoms for flexible adaptation. Organizational policies must encompass diverse entities ranging from supply-chain participants to nation-state collaborators to military units in command centers and in the field. They must define legal, contractual, and economic structures and responsibilities for all participants. Technical policies must prescribe architectural frameworks, design rules, semantic structures, and development environments as the rules of participation and the context for freedom of action in evolving and adapting ULS systems. And operational policies must define usage authorizations, responsibilities, and security processes across a broad spectrum of stakeholders ranging from software developers to national governments. A major research challenge is to characterize the options available for governing ULS systems, including methods derived from principles of democracy, collaborative teaming, motivational competition, hierarchical delegation, and economic self-interest.

Policy Content for Local Evolution. Because of their scale and longevity, ULS systems will experience and should create incentives for substantial local adaptation and bottom-up evolution. Studies are needed to understand why and how end users make local adaptations to systems. We need research on how to develop policies for guiding system evolution when local needs must be met but conflict with global policies. Local stakeholders may have little choice in addressing urgent needs, for example, in responding to tactical situations or isolating failed parts of systems, and ULS system policies must accommodate and adapt to such situations. Research in mechanism design (described in Section 6.2.1) is an example of a promising approach for determining supportive policies in this context.

Computational Automation for Policy Decisions. The scope and scale of ULS systems will require that policy mechanisms be automated. Research is required in collaborative work environments for policy formulation and conflict resolution, techniques for evaluating the semantic consistency of policies across cultures and languages, methods for rapid assessment of policy conformance and application of permissions or sanctions, and incorporation of timely feedback and local policy modifications in response to changing tactical needs.

6.7.2 Fast Acquisition for ULS Systems

Research Tracks

Essential	Support
M1 (RT2)	M1 (RT1)
M3 (RT5)	

The pervasive application of ULS systems to support global operations in many simultaneous strategic and tactical situations will generate many requirements for rapid evolution to meet changing threats and environments. Research will be needed in the following topics to achieve this level of flexibility:

New Acquisition Processes for Fast Response. Current methods of system acquisition based on requests for proposals (RFPs) and lengthy vendor evaluations could impose unacceptable delays in the development and evolution of ULS systems. Research is required to create new acquisition models that enable rapid responses. In particular, much of the evolution of ULS systems will occur in situ, thereby imposing requirements to maintain critical operational capabilities while adding or improving other capabilities in place. Present acquisition methods that assume traditional life-cycle models for development and testing prior to deployment are ill suited to such a dynamic environment. This research must address contracting, intellectual property, information sharing, and security across supply-chain organizations.

Integrating Supply Chains for Operational Readiness. Research is needed to understand how supply-chain organizations could be integrated as first-class operational components into ULS ecosystems, to enable the continual communication, knowledge acquisition, and training necessary for fast responses to changing system requirements. Such a strategy would integrate engineering capabilities for system evolution with DoD capabilities for system use and would put developers on the critical path when rapid adaptation is required for mission success. In such an environment, supply-chain organizations ranging from established vendors to open-source collaborations could undergo periodic assessment of capabilities, participate in joint training and readiness exercises with the forces, and come and go as needs and capabilities change.

Capitalizing on Ad Hoc Acquisition. It may often be the case that, to meet immediate needs, local users of ULS systems will be forced to engage in ad hoc acquisition of components whose functionality and quality properties are not well understood or trusted. Because these components address unforeseen problems, an opportunity will arise to improve and generalize their application across similar environments. Research is required on ad hoc acquisition to better understand how it can affect global system integrity and potentially augment system capabilities.

Computational Automation for Fast Acquisition. Speed in acquisition will depend on automated processing of organizational agreements, system requirements, work-product integration, and status tracking and reporting. Research is needed to create the information models, computational processes, and training that can support this level of automation.

> Integrated Supply Chains for Operational Readiness

Relevance to DoD Missions.
ULS systems will be required to adapt to changing missions and unanticipated circumstances encountered by warfighters. Quick reaction to field new capabilities will require software-acquisition and development processes at all levels capable of fast and dependable responses to these changing needs.

Key Concepts.
Integrated supply chains are an approach to operational readiness that treats suppliers as intrinsic, first-class components of ULS systems. In this model, suppliers ranging from established vendors to open-source communities to individual entrepreneurs are pre-qualified in terms of available resources and demonstrated capabilities, and are pre-positioned in terms of contracting, information sharing, and security relationships to enable fast response to operational needs as they arise. Readiness teams within supply chains monitor ULS systems, engage in simulations, and train with the forces to prepare for fast evolution of software capabilities to meet tactical needs. The integrated supply-chain approach can benefit from automated systems that support fast acquisition as well as from ULS systems with designed-in facilities for rapid evolution.

6.7.3 Management of ULS Systems

Research Tracks

Essential

(M1) (RT1)

(M2) (RT3)

(M3) (RT6)

ULS systems will be designed to support dynamic coalitions and management of tactical and strategic operations through linkage of field units with command-and-control functions on any scale necessary. At the same time, the size and highly distributed nature of ULS systems will limit global visibility and decentralize system management within an overall framework of organizational, technical, and operational policies. Research is required on how to structure ULS system management in the following areas:

Managing ULS Systems for Operational Readiness. The overarching requirement for ULS systems is operational readiness at all times under all conditions. While the systems will be subject to persistent failures and permanent risks of intrusion and compromise, sufficient resources must always be available to meet immediate operational needs. Research is required to understand how to plan, acquire, and organize system resources under adverse conditions to achieve this goal in a decentralized management structure.

Managing ULS Ecosystems for Fast Evolution. The supply chains of vendors and integrators that will populate ULS ecosystems must be organized, and incentives must be provided to evolve ULS system capabilities at a rapid pace in response to changing operational needs. Research is required to understand how to manage these organizations, ranging from large and established contractors to open-source communities and individual entrepreneurs, to achieve a level of cooperation and collaboration that can satisfy requirements for fast system evolution.

Managing ULS System Research for New Capabilities. The national importance of ULS systems and the demanding problems they pose will encourage a rich infrastructure of research and graduate education. This infrastructure should be encouraged and supported to develop new capabilities for ULS systems as they grow and evolve over time. Research is required to develop management strategies for ensuring that ULS system research programs are properly focused and produce results that accumulate into significant operational capabilities. At the same time, it is important to foster a new generation of ULS system experts and practitioners through graduate education programs.

Managing ULS System Knowledge to Guide Evolution. ULS systems engineering development and operational use will generate knowledge that can be preserved and analyzed to guide future evolution. Research is required to understand how to manage the acquisition, preservation, and analysis of this rich body of information.

6.7.4 Further Reading

The seminal discussion of wicked problems can be found in Rittel and Webber's "Dilemmas in a general theory of planning" [Rittel 73]. Methods for interorganizational supply-chain collaboration and cycle-time reduction are discussed by Handfield and Nichols [Handfield 02]. Important perspectives for ULS supply-chain management are provided by Baldwin and her colleagues [Baldwin 00]: appropriate definition of system modularity is identified as a driving force in supply-chain integration, innovation, and efficiency; and managing supply chains for speed is discussed as a competitive advantage. A management perspective on how to achieve resiliency in large-scale systems and enterprises under adverse conditions is provided by Sheffi [Sheffi 05].

[Baldwin 00] Baldwin, C.; Clark, K.; Magretta, J.; Dyer, J.; Fisher, M.; & Fites, D. *Harvard Business Review on Managing the Value Chain.* Boston, MA: Harvard Business School Publishing, 2000.

[Handfield 02] Handfield. R. & Nichols, E. *Supply Chain Redesign: Transforming Supply Chains into Integrated Value Systems.* Upper Saddle River, NJ: Financial Times Prentice Hall, 2002.

[Rittel 73] Rittel, H. & Webber, M. "Dilemmas in a general theory of planning." *Policy Sciences* 4 (1973): 155–169.

[Sheffi 05] Sheffi, Y. *The Resilient Enterprise: Overcoming Vulnerability for Competitive Advantage.* Boston, MA: MIT Press, 2005.

Glossary

A

abstraction: 1. A process of eliminating, hiding, or ignoring characteristics or aspects of a concept unrelated to a given purpose. 2. A concept or system construct that has been subjected to a process of abstraction.

acceptability-oriented computing: An approach to the construction of systems in which a designer identifies a set of properties that the execution must satisfy to be acceptable to its users. This is in contrast to the traditional approach, which is to construct a system with as few errors as possible. Acceptability-oriented computing was defined by Martin Rinard, Professor of Computer Science at MIT, in the paper, "Acceptability Oriented Computing," presented at the 2003 Object-Oriented Systems, Languages, & Applications Conference (OOPSLA '03).

agile method or ***agile methodology:*** A style of software development characterized by its release schedule, attitude toward change, and patterns of communication. The product is developed in iterations, usually one to four weeks long. At the end of each iteration, the product has additional, fully implemented value and is ready to be deployed. The design horizon usually extends only to the end of the current iteration; little code is written in anticipation of future needs. The project is seen by the programmers as a stream of unanticipated requirements. Written natural-language communication is considered a usually inefficient compromise. Face-to-face communication is higher bandwidth (but transient). Executable documentation—code and tests—is permanent, less ambiguous, and self-checking. Agile projects prefer a combination of the latter two over the first.

aleatoric: Pertaining to luck, chance, or randomness.

allopoiesis: A process whereby an organization or network of components produces something other than itself; literally, *other-production*. An example of allopoiesis is an assembly line.

annealing: Any process for increasing the order of a system by first increasing its susceptibility to disorder and then steadily decreasing such susceptibility in the presence of mechanisms or phenomena that tend to create or capture order.

ant-colony optimization: A technique for solving problems that can be reduced to finding short paths in a graph by using a process similar to how an ant colony finds paths to food. In this process, individuals randomly wander the graph, leaving behind a trail that dissipates over time. When a good path is found, the individual returns along the left trail, reinforcing it. Other individuals who find this path are likely to follow it, further reinforcing it. Because trails dissipate over time, longer trails will be less likely to be reinforced than shorter ones.

aspect-oriented programming: A programming paradigm that attempts to aid programmers in the separation of concerns (breaking down a program into distinct parts that overlap in functionality as little as possible). The hallmark of the paradigm is to represent as modules ***crosscutting concerns***, which are distinct design decisions or functionality that are conceptually distinct but whose implementations are usually dispersed throughout the modules of a system. The idea was first presented in the paper, "Aspect-Oriented Programming," by Gregor Kiczales, John Lamping, Anurag Mendhekar, Chris Maeda, Cristina Lopes, Jean-Marc Loingtier, and John Irwin, published in the *Proceedings of the European Conference on Object-Oriented Programming*, 1997.

attribute-specific design rule: A ***design rule*** aimed at maintaining a particular ***quality attribute.***

augmented reality: A view of the real environment augmented with computationally supplied information, providing a composite view of the world that is partly real and partly digital. A military heads-up display is a simple example of augmented reality.

autocatalysis: A chemical reaction whose products include catalysts for that reaction.

autopoiesis: A process whereby an organization or network of components produces itself; literally, *self-production*. An example of autopoiesis is a cell or an organism.

B

Bayesian technique: Any learning or decision-making technique that relies on Bayes' Theorem which, informally, tells how to update or revise beliefs in light of new evidence.

belief logic: Any logical calculus that models belief; for example, as sets of formulae or ***probabilistically***.

black-box abstraction: An abstraction or component whose implementation is hidden and whose functionality is available only through its interface (cf., ***open abstraction).***

black-box testing: *Black-box testing*, *concrete-box testing*, and *functional testing* refer to testing the outputs of a program given knowledge of only its functional specification and not its implementation. Black-box testing is in contrast to ***clear-box testing.***

C

certification: Declaration via a formal certificate from an accredited body attesting that a particular assurance regarding software, hardware, or a system is true.

cleanroom software engineering: A software-development methodology defined by Harlan Mills and his colleagues, based on formal methods, iterative implementation, and statistical quality control. The objectives of the cleanroom process are to develop software incrementally, produce software that approaches zero defects prior to first execution, and certify software fitness for use. See *Cleanroom Software Engineering: Technology and Process* by S. Prowell, C. Trammell, R. Linger, and J. Poore. Reading, MA: Addison Wesley Longman, 1999.

clear-box testing: *White-box testing*, *clear-box testing*, *glass-box testing*, and *structural testing* refer to testing the outputs of a program given knowledge of how the program is implemented. Clear-box testing is generally done by programmers who try to cover parts of the code and cases that they suspect are prone to coding errors. Clear-box testing is in contrast to ***black-box testing***.

competitive software design: A design process in which competition is intentionally introduced at many levels.

complexity science: A scientific discipline that studies systems of multiple, possibly diverse, interconnected elements that have the capacity to change in response to experience, both external and internal.

composition: An act or result of combining simpler objects into more complex ones. For example, simpler data types can be combined into more complex ones. Composition also refers to the act or result of determining the net effect produced by combining functions; for example a composite function can be determined by applying each given function to the results of the previous function in some order in a cascade.

concurrent: When the execution flow of several computational processes are able to run simultaneously, perhaps while sharing resources. In general, concurrent execution is not expected to save elapsed time over sequential execution (cf., ***parallel).***

context-aware assistive computing or ***context-aware computing:*** An approach to the design of a pervasive or ***ubiquitous computing*** system that focuses on the shared understanding between humans and their computational environments, particularly regarding their shared context. Context is any information that can be used to characterize the situation of entities (i.e., people, places, and objects) that is relevant to the interaction between a user and a system, including the user and the system themselves. Context is typically the location, identity, and state of people, groups, and computational and physical objects.

contract net: A collection of computational nodes that collaborate to solve a distributed problem by allocating tasks to nodes via a series of contract negotiations using a formal protocol consisting of task annoucements, bids, awards, and results reporting. Negotiations involve task descriptions and requirements such as mandatory available resources and time constraints. The concept was first introduced by Reid Smith and Randy Davis in "The Contract Net Protocol: High level Communication and Control in a

Distributed Problem Solver," *IEEE Transactions on Computers 29,* 12 (1980):1104-1113.

CORBA: **C**ommon **O**bject **R**equest **B**roker **A**rchitecture (CORBA) is a standard for software components. It defines application programming interfaces (APIs), communication protocols, and object/service information models to enable heterogeneous applications written in various languages running on various platforms to interoperate. CORBA thus provides platform and location transparency for sharing objects across a distributed computing platform.

crosscutting or ***crosscutting concerns:*** A single, coherent design or implementation decision or issue whose implementation typically must be scattered throughout the modules of a system. A crosscutting concern is called an aspect in ***aspect-oriented programming.***

crossover: A genetic operator in ***digital software evolution*** that varies the genetic makeup of a member of the next generation by taking genetic contributions from two members of the current generation. In a ***genetic algorithm***, genetic material is represented linearly, and crossover is via a form of splicing. In genetic programming, genetic material is represented as a tree or as trees, and crossover is via a form of subtree substitution.

cryptographic: Referring to the security of information based on encoding messages in such a way that they cannot be decoded without special, private, and hard-to-acquire information.

cybernetics: The science of systems of control and communications in living organisms and machines.

D

decentralized system: A ***distributed system*** with no central authority for any of its aspects.

Dempster-Shafer theory: A formal theory of evidence (see ***evidence theory***) based on belief functions and plausible reasoning that is used to combine separate pieces of information (evidence) to calculate the probability of an event. The theory was developed by Arthur P. Dempster and Glenn Shafer.

design architecture: A set of decisions that partitions the task of producing the complete design for a system into a set of largely separable subtasks.

design of all levels: An approach to architecture and design that includes as part of the design not only the artifact being constructed but also the organizational, social, and process structure of the design teams, including individuals, firms, and other organizations.

design risk: A design decision made in the absence of certainty of the outcome. In some design contexts, it is not always known whether a decision will result in a satisfactory artifact when the design is completed and implemented; such a decision represents a risk in the design process that must be assessed and managed.

design rule: A decision concerning the architecture of a system that helps establish the degree and nature of the modularity of the system's design. Typically, a design rule minimizes interaction between modules in the design as well as between different designers or design groups; design rules are also typically based on design experience. For example, the decision whether to control the screen of a computer with the CPU or a separate graphics processor is a design rule that structures the design space for a computer.

design space: The set of design parameters along with the range of values for those parameters for a design. A design can be considered an outline for an artifact (its architecture) along with a set of decisions about the nature and details of the outline; the space of possible decisions is the design space.

deterministic: A property of a computation that always has one (and the same) result given the same initial state and inputs.

digital evolution or ***digital software evolution:*** An automated methodology inspired by biological evolution to create software that best performs a specified task. It is a ***machine learning*** technique that uses an evolutionary algorithm (i.e., a ***genetic algorithm*** or ***genetic programming***) to optimize a population of programs according to a ***fitness function*** that measures a program's ability to perform a specified task.

dissipative system: An open system that is operating outside equilibrium within an environment that exchanges energy, matter, or ***entropy***.

distributed cognition: A branch of cognitive science that proposes that human cognition is not confined to the individual, but is distributed by attaching memories, facts, or knowledge to objects, individuals, and tools in the environment.

distributed system: A system in which there are a number of components communicating over a network that are trying to cooperate in some fashion (or which taken together form the system).

distribution: Placing execution flows in different processes or on different computational ***platforms.*** Distribution is typically applied to improve fault tolerance or to access remote resources.

domain-specific language: A programming language designed to be useful for a specific set of tasks.

driven system: A system with external energy or information inputs.

E

econometrics: The application of statistical and mathematical methods in the field of economics to describe the numeric relationships between key economic forces. The main purpose of econometrics is to empirically verify economic theory.

ecosystem: In biology, an ecosystem is a community of plants, animals, and microorganisms that are linked by energy and nutrient flows and that interact with each other and with the physical environment. Rain forests, deserts, coral reefs, grasslands, and a rotting log are all examples of ecosystems. ULS systems can be characterized as ***socio-technical ecosystems.***

embodied interaction: A form of interaction with a computational system that reflects the philosophy that effective communication must take place in physical and social environments, not purely in virtual ones.

embodied virtuality: The manifestation of the results, processes, and mechanisms of computation in the physical world. This term, first defined by Mark Weiser in *The Computer for the 21st Century* (San Francisco, CA: Morgan Kauffman Publishers, 1995) is an alternative to *ubiquitous computing*, which envisions computers as physical presences in numerous parts of the real world.

Enterprise JavaBeans: A component architecture for building distributed, object-oriented business applications in Java. An Enterprise JavaBean (EJB) encapsulates business logic in a component framework that manages the details of ***security,*** transaction, and state management. Low-level details such as multi-threading, resource pooling, clustering, distributed naming, automatic persistence, remote invocation, transaction boundary management, and distributed transaction management are handled by the EJB "container."

entropy: Informally, the degree of disorder of a system. Entropy has specific definitions beyond the scope of this glossary in thermodynamics, statistical mechanics, and information theory.

epistemic uncertainty: Uncertainty based on lack of knowledge.

evidence theory: A formal system of reasoning about knowledge based on a belief function (not defined in this glossary) as the representation of degree of belief, and a method of combining evidence and belief. The theory is explained in *A Mathematical Theory of Evidence* by Glenn Shafer (Princeton, NJ: Princeton University Press, 1976).

example-driven design: A variant of ***test-driven design*** in which the tests are written as if they were a series of examples being used to teach someone how to use the code, beginning with simple cases and moving toward the trickier ones.

F

fitness function: A type of ***objective function*** that quantifies the optimality of a solution in a ***genetic algorithm*** so that a solution can be ranked against all the others.

flow-structure analysis: A method for understanding the compositions of system services implemented in a network to carry out user tasks. See *Flow-Service-Quality (FSQ) Engineering: Foundations for Network System Analysis and Development*, by R. Linger, M. Pleszkoch, G.

Walton, and A. Hevner (CMU/SEI-2002-TN-019), Software Engineering Institute, Carnegie Mellon University, Pittsburgh, PA, June 2002.

fractal: Informally, a shape that appears similar at all scales; formally, a geometric object whose Hausdorff dimension (not defined in this glossary) is greater than its topological dimension (not defined in this glossary).

function extraction (FX): Technology for automated computation of the net functional effect, or behavior, of programs, presented in terms of behavior catalogs for human understanding and analysis. See *The Impact of Function Extraction Technology on Next-Generation Software Engineering* by A. Hevner, R. Linger, R. Collins, M. Pleszkoch, S. Prowell, and G. Walton (CMU/SEI 2005-TR-015), Software Engineering Institute, Carnegie Mellon University, Pittsburgh, PA, July 2005.

function-theoretic: Of or referring to ***function-theoretic foundations***.

function-theoretic foundations: An approach to formalizing computation based on a view of programs as implementations of mathematical functions or relations, regardless of their subject matter or language. Function-theoretic foundations provide methods for software specification, design, verification, and analysis, and play a key role in ***cleanroom software engineering, function-theoretic verification***, and ***function extraction.***

fuzzy set: A set with imprecise membership criteria. In classical set theory, a set can be defined by a characteristic function that takes an element of the universe and assigns 1 if the element belongs to the set and 0 otherwise. A fuzzy set is defined by a membership function that assigns a real number in the interval [0,1], where 1 means the element belongs, 0 means it doesn't, and a number in between 0 and 1 indicates the degree of membership. This number is not a probability or likelihood, but an imprecision or vagueness. For example, a person walking through the doorway between the kitchen and dining room whose foot is in the dining room and part of whose body is in the kitchen is partly in the set of people in the kitchen and partly in the set of people in the dining room.

G

game theory: A branch of applied mathematics that studies strategic situations in which players choose actions in an attempt to maximize their returns.

genetic algorithm: A method of simulating the action of evolution within a computer. A population is evolved by employing ***crossover*** and mutation operators along with a ***fitness function*** that determines how likely individuals are to reproduce. A genetic algorithm usually operates on a population of fixed-length vectors of characteristics.

genetic programming: A form of ***genetic algorithm*** in which members of the evolving population are tree-like representations of computer programs.

glue or ***glue code:*** Code that enables one piece of code or a component to interact with other code or another component.

GOMS model: A description of the knowledge that a person must have to carry out tasks on a device or system. The acronym "GOMS" stands for **G**oals, **O**perators, **M**ethods, and **S**election rules. A GOMS model consists of descriptions of the methods needed to accomplish specified goals. The methods are a series of steps consisting of operators that the person performs. A method may call for sub-goals to be accomplished, so the methods have a hierarchical structure. If there is more than one method to accomplish a goal, then the GOMS model includes *selection rules* that choose the appropriate method depending on the context. The GOMS framework was proposed by Card, Moran, and Newell in *The Psychology of Human-Computer Interaction* (Mahwah, NJ: Lawrence Erlbaum Associates, 1983).

greedy algorithm: A problem-solving or optimization algorithm that uses the ***metaheuristic*** of making the locally optimum choice at each stage until the entire problem is solved or optimization is complete. It typically produces a good solution quickly but rarely an optimum one.

H

hybrid systems modeling: The process of and languages for modeling and simulating systems with both continuous and discrete processes. Hybrid systems modeling aims to model systems that can be described by ordinary differential equations, partial differential equations, differential algebraic equations, and ordinary differential equations interfaced with discrete-time algorithms.

hypermutation: A biological process or mechanism to enable rapid adaptation to environmental conditions (including parasites and viruses) by altering (usually accelerating) rates of mutation. For example, the acquired immune system in multicellular animals uses hypermutation.

I

in situ control and adaptation: A model-based approach for designing adaptive quality of service in ***distributed systems.***

in situ control, reflection, and adaptation: in situ control and adaptation using ***reflection*** as an approach.

Internet storm: A disruptive and sometimes malicious set of time-localized, large-scale Internet infrastructure events. Denial-of-service attacks, Internet worms, and cascading router failures are examples of Internet storms.

J

jitter: A slight random or irregular variation in an otherwise regular sequence or signal. In telecommunication, an abrupt variation of one or more signal characteristics, such as the interval between successive pulses, the amplitude of successive cycles, or the frequency or phase of successive cycles. In packet-based networking, jitter is the variation in the delay of packets.

L

latency: A time delay between the moment something is initiated and the moment its first effect begins.

law of large numbers: A statistical law stating that the average of a random sample from a large population is likely to be close to the mean of that population.

M

machine learning: An approach to certain computations in which, broadly speaking, a computer changes its own structure, program, or data based on inputs or external data in such a manner that its expected future performance improves. More specifically, machine learning refers to a set of techniques such as automatic rule extraction and application, determining statistical characteristics of a population and using them to make decisions, determining the weights and perhaps topology for a neural net based on positive and negative training examples and using it for classification, etc.

mechanism design: A sub-field of ***game theory*** that studies how to design the rules of a game to achieve a specific outcome by setting up a structure in which each player has an incentive to behave as the designer intends. One branch of mechanism design is the creation of markets such as auctions.

metadata: Data that are about or that describe data. Note that the word "metadata" has been trademarked by The Metadata Company, and the legal status of the generic use of the term has not been settled.

metaheuristics: High-level procedures that coordinate simple heuristics, such as local search, to find solutions that are of better quality than those found by the simple heuristics alone; metaheuristics are typically used in situations where exact algorithms are not feasible. Metaheuristics include ***simulated annealing, genetic algorithms,*** tabu search, GRASP, scatter search, ***ant-colony optimization,*** variable neighborhood search, and their hybrids.

metastability: The ability of a non-equilibrium state to persist for some period of time. A system in a metastable state is able to pass to a more stable equilibrium when sufficiently disturbed.

microeconomics: The branch of economics that deals with small-scale economic factors, such as the economics of an individual firm, product, or consumer rather than with the aggregate. One of the goals of microeconomics is to analyze market mechanisms that establish relative prices and allocate resources.

middleware: A set of layers and components that provides reusable common services and network programming mechanisms. Middleware resides on top of an operating system and its protocol stacks but below the structure and functionality of any particular application.

model checking: A method to algorithmically verify a design by checking whether a model derived from the design satisfies its formal specification.

model-driven architecture: An approach to model-driven engineering architecture sponsored by the Object Management Group that provides a set of guidelines for structuring specifications expressed as models. System functionality is defined as a platform-independent model (PIM) through an appropriate ***domain-specific language.*** Given a platform definition model (PDM) corresponding to ***CORBA***, ***.NET***, etc., the PIM is then translated to one or more platform-specific models (PSMs) for the actual implementation. The translations between the PIM and PSMs are normally performed using automated tools.

monoculture: A system with low diversity.

monotonic: The property of a type of information and a method of reasoning or operating on it for which the addition of new information does not decrease the set of valid inferences or operations.

multi-valued logic: A logical calculus in which there are more than two possible truth values. Examples include fuzzy logic and ***probabilistic*** logic such as ***Dempster-Shafer theory.***

mutator function: As used in a ***metaheuristic*** process, a function that takes a current state and returns a neighbor state, typically in a ***probabilistic*** manner.

N

.NET: The Microsoft .NET Framework is a component of the Microsoft Windows operating system. It provides a large body of pre-coded solutions to common program requirements and manages the execution of programs written specifically for the framework. Programs written for the .NET framework execute in a software environment that manages the program's runtime requirements. This runtime environment, which is also a part of the .NET framework, is known as the Common Language Runtime (CLR). The CLR provides the appearance of an application virtual machine.

neuro-evolution: The use of ***genetic algorithms*** to create an operational artificial neural network. The term is used ambiguously in the literature to refer both to systems that evolve only the values of the connection weights for a network of pre-specified topology as well as to systems that evolve the topology of the network in addition to the weights.

nondeterministic: A property of a computation that may have more than one result. One way to implement a nondeterministic algorithm is using backtracking; another is to explore (all) possible solutions in parallel.

non-monotonic: The property of a type of information and a method of reasoning or operating on it that the addition of new information may decrease the set of valid inferences or operations; not ***monotonic.***

NP-complete: A decision problem that requires a ***nondeterministic,*** polynomial-time (NP) algorithm to solve; an NP-complete problem is among the most difficult-to-solve NP problems. Formally, a decision problem is NP-complete if it is in NP (requires a nondeterministic, polynomial-time algorithm to solve), and every other problem in NP is reducible to it.

n-version programming: A software-development strategy to increase reliability through redundancy. One approach is to create (possibly independently) multiple versions of a component and to combine their results.

O

objective function: A function to be minimized or maximized in a ***metaheuristic*** optimization process.

off-the-shelf components: Components designed and implemented for specific purposes but with no specific application in mind; such components can be used in a variety of applications, sometimes with external scaffolding. A program library is an example.

open abstraction: An abstraction or component whose implementation can be customized or augmented.

orchestration: The activities needed to make the elements of a system work together in sufficient harmony to ensure continuous satisfaction of a set of specified objectives.

P

parallel: When the execution flows of several computational processes are able to run simultaneously, typically with little or no resource sharing. In general, parallel execution is expected to save elapsed time over sequential execution (cf., ***concurrent).***

particle swarm optimization: A problem-solving ***metaheuristic*** that mimics the behavior of a flock or swarm. A population of individuals seeking to find the most fit location is placed randomly in a multidimensional search space. Each individual flies through the space with a velocity that is updated according to a linear combination of the current velocity, a vector toward the most fit location that the individual has seen so far, and a vector toward the most fit location seen so far either by nearby individuals (in one variation of the algorithm) or by the entire flock (in another). The latter two vectors are combined with independent random scalars. The process terminates when the location with the best fitness exceeds a given threshold.

pattern: A description of a particular recurring design problem that arises in specific design contexts along with a well-proven solution for that problem. In some cases, the solution is specified by describing its constituent participants, their responsibilities and relationships, and the ways in which they collaborate.

phase transition: A process by which a system changes from one state to another with different properties, sometimes as a result of small changes.

phenotropics: A mechanism for component interaction that uses pattern recognition or artificial cognition in place of function invocation or message passing. The term was coined by Jaron Lanier. See John Brockman, *The Next Fifty Years: Science in the First Half of the Twenty-first Century*, Vintage, 2002.

platform: The combination of hardware and software that provides a virtual machine that executes software and applications. Software platforms include operating systems, libraries, and frameworks.

possibility theory: A mathematical theory for dealing with particular types of uncertainty as an alternative to probability theory. Possibility theory was defined by Lotfi Zadeh in 1978 as an extension to his theory of ***fuzzy sets*** and fuzzy logic.

probabilistic: Pertaining to any method, approach, or form of reasoning that relies on probability or theories of likelihood (cf., ***stochastic).***

proof-carrying code: A technique for safe execution of untrusted code. A code receiver establishes a set of safety rules that guarantee safe behavior of programs, and the code producer creates a formal safety proof. The receiver can use a proof validator to check that the proof is valid.

Q

quality attribute: A property of a system by which its quality will be judged by some stakeholder or stakeholders. Quality-attribute requirements such as those for performance, security, modifiability, reliability, and usability have a significant influence on the architecture of a system.

quality of service: The probability that a system will deliver particular levels of measurable computational and communication properties such as availability, bandwidth, ***latency,*** and ***jitter.*** Policies and mechanisms typically are designed to control and improve the quality of service of a system.

quasi-stability: The ability of a non-equilibrium state to be long lasting but not perpetual; ***metastability***.

R

recovery-oriented programming: An approach to software reliability that focuses on recovering from faults quickly and effectively. This approach was devised by David Patterson and his colleagues (*Recovery Oriented Computing (ROC): Motivation, Definition, Techniques, and Case Studies*, Computer Science Technical

Report UCB//CSD-02-1175, University of California at Berkeley, March 15, 2002).

refactor: The process of rewriting software to improve its readability or structure while retaining its meaning or behavior.

reflection: A computational process that is able to reason about itself.

requirements drift: A slow variation in the requirements for a system as conditions change, including as a result of experience with the system or as the set of stakeholders changes.

revelation principle: The principle in ***game theory*** or ***mechanism design*** that states that for any equilibrium (stable state) of a game of incomplete information, there corresponds an associated revelation mechanism that has an equilibrium where the players truthfully report their payoff-related, private information.

robust; robustness: The ability of a system to continue to function despite the existence of faults in its component subsystems, parts, or communication mechanisms.

S

satisfice: To seek a solution that satisfies the minimum requirements necessary.

security: The capability of a system to provide confidentiality, integrity, and availability of data and services, both locally and globally.

self-organizing criticality: A ***driven system*** that radically changes its behavior or structure because of its intrinsic dynamics. The archetype of a self-organized critical system is a sand pile. Sand is slowly dropped onto a surface, forming a pile. As the pile grows, avalanches occur that carry sand from the top to the bottom of the pile.

sequence-based specification: A method of specification distinguished by a process of enumerating all stimulus-response pairs as well as all sequences of stimuli along with their required responses, including whether a sequence is not possible, and the identification of equivalence classes of sequences. The method is described in "Sequence-Based Specification of Deterministic Systems," by S. Prowell and J. Poore, *Software - Practice and Experience 28*, 3 (Mar 1998): 329-344.

service-oriented architecture: A design for linking computational resources (principally, applications and data) on demand using standardized (typically network-based) interfaces and protocols to achieve the desired results for service consumers (which can be end users or other services).

simulated annealing: A problem-solving or optimization ***metaheuristic*** that finds a good approximation to a global optimum by using a process inspired by metallurgical ***annealing***. It operates by repeatedly considering a random nearby solution, and selecting that solution with a probability that depends on the difference between the current fitness and desired fitness, and on a global temperature that decreases according to a schedule. The process terminates after, at most, a fixed number of steps.

socio-technical ecosystem: An ***ecosystem*** whose elements are groups of people together with their computational and physical environments.

speciation: The formation of new and distinct species in a process of natural or ***digital evolution***.

staged computation: Breaking the construction of a program into stages whose outputs are programs. *Partial evaluation* is an example of staged computation.

statistical mechanics: The branch of physics that makes theoretical predictions about the behavior of a macroscopic system on the basis of statistical laws governing its component particles.

stochastic: Involving chance or probability; involving or containing a random variable or variables. For example, a stochastic process is one whose behavior is ***nondeterministic*** in that the next state of the environment is partially but not fully determined by the previous state of the environment.

swarm intelligence: The collective behavior of decentralized, self-organized systems. Swarm-intelligence systems are typically made up of a population of simple agents interacting locally with one another and with their environment. Local interactions between such agents often lead to the emergence of global behavior. Examples from nature include ant colonies, bird flocking, animal herding, bacteria molding, and fish schooling.

system health: A measure of the ability of a system to deliver its required functionality at its specified quality levels.

system of systems: A system comprising independent, self-contained systems that, taken as a whole, satisfy a specified need.

system viability: The success or continuing effectiveness of a system.

T

test-driven design: A style of program design that begins by writing one simple test, then writing just enough code to pass it. Then another simple test is written, and code is added to pass both it and the previous test. The programmer then looks for opportunities to improve the code by generalizing it, removing duplication, restructuring it, or making it more understandable. The test-code-improve cycle repeats until there are no more tests to be had. It is claimed that a good global design emerges from the need to decouple the code to make tests run fast and the local heuristic rules for code improvement. The tests are retained and run frequently to prevent unintended effects of changes to the design.

trust: The extent to which users of a system can rely on its data and services.

type-safe staged computation: A ***staged computation*** using a language that guarantees that every generated program is type safe.

U

ubiquitous computing: The integration of computation into the environment; this is in contrast to computers as distinct objects.

ultra-large-scale (ULS) system: A system at least one of whose dimensions is of such a large scale that constructing the system using development processes and techniques prevailing at the start of the 21st century is problematic. ULS systems exhibit the following characteristics: decentralization; conflicting, unknowable, and diverse requirements; continuous evolution and deployment; heterogeneous and changing elements; erosion of the people/system boundary; and normal failures of parts of the system.

universal usability: The characteristic of an information or communications device that it is usable by any person regardless of skill level, knowledge, age, gender, disabilities, disabling conditions (mobility, sunlight, noise), literacy, culture, income, etc., and regardless of the number of (simultaneous) users.

user-centered design: A design philosophy and process in which the needs, wants, and limitations of the end user of an interface or artifact are given extensive attention at each stage of the design process.

V

validation, software: Confirmation by examination and provision of objective evidence that software specifications conform to user needs and intended uses and that the requirements implemented through software can be consistently fulfilled.

verification, software: Evidence that a design meets all of its specified requirements.

Von Neumann execution model: A model of computation consisting of a central processing unit (CPU) and a single memory for instructions and data.

W

wicked problem: An ill-defined design and planning problem having incomplete, contradictory, and changing requirements. Solutions to wicked problems are often difficult to recognize because of complex interdependencies. This term was suggested by H. Rittel and M. Webber in the paper, "Dilemmas in a General Theory of Planning," *Policy Sciences 4*, Elsevier Scientific Publishing Company, Inc., Amsterdam, 1973.